# READING
## AND THE
## LAW

Edited by
## Robert J. Harper II
Lawyer's Committee for Civil Rights Under Law
## Gary Kilarr
Virginia Polytechnic Institute and State University

International Reading Association
800 Barksdale Road, Newark, Delaware 19711

Clearinghouse on Reading and Communication Skills
1111 Kenyon Road, Urbana, Illinois 61801

The International Reading Association attempts, through its publications, to provide a forum for a wide spectrum of opinion on reading. This policy permits divergent viewpoints without assuming the endorsement of the Association.

ERIC/RCS Staff Editor: Karen Steiner
Published in April 1978

ERIC Clearinghouse on Reading and Communication Skills
1111 Kenyon Road, Urbana, Illinois 61801

International Reading Association
800 Barksdale Road, Newark, Delaware 19711

Printed in the United States of America

The material in this publication was prepared pursuant to a contract with the National Institute of Education, U.S. Department of Health, Education and Welfare. Contractors undertaking such projects under government sponsorship are encouraged to express freely their judgment in professional and technical matters. Prior to publication, the manuscript was submitted to the International Reading Association for critical review and determination of professional competence. This publication has met such standards. Points of view or opinions, however, do not necessarily represent the official view or opinions of either the International Reading Association or the National Institute of Education.

**Library of Congress Cataloging in Publication Data**
Main entry under title:

Reading and the law.

   Bibliography: p.
   1. Reading—Law and legislation—United States—
Addresses, essays, lectures.  I. Harper, Robert James,
1949–  II. Kilarr, Gary.  III. International Reading
Association.
KF4203.5.A75R4      344'.73'077      78-6213
ISBN 0-87207-854-X

# CONTENTS

# FOREWORD

The Educational Resources Information Center (ERIC) is a national information system developed by the U.S. Office of Education and now sponsored by the National Institute of Education (NIE). It provides ready access to descriptions of exemplary programs, research and development efforts, and related information useful in developing more effective educational programs.

Through its network of specialized centers or clearinghouses, each of which is responsible for a particular educational area, ERIC acquires, evaluates, abstracts, and indexes current significant information and lists this information in its reference publications.

ERIC/RCS, the ERIC Clearinghouse on Reading and Communication Skills, disseminates educational information related to research, instruction, and personnel preparation at all levels and in all institutions. The scope of interest of the Clearinghouse includes relevant research reports, literature reviews, curriculum guides and descriptions, conference papers, project or program reviews, and other print materials related to all aspects of reading, English, educational journalism, and speech communication.

The ERIC system has already made available—through the ERIC Document Reproduction Service—much informative data. However, if the findings of specific educational research are to be intelligible to teachers and applicable to teaching, considerable bodies of data must be reevaluated, focused, translated, and molded into an essentially different context. Rather than resting at the point of making research reports readily accessible, NIE has directed the separate clearinghouses to work with professional organizations in developing information analysis papers in specific areas within the scope of the clearinghouses.

ERIC/RCS is pleased to cooperate with the International Reading Association in making *Reading and the Law* available to the members of IRA.

Bernard O'Donnell
Director, ERIC/RCS

# INTRODUCTION

The effective use and understanding of the language processes—reading, writing, speaking, and listening—is essential for survival in today's society. The acquisition of a driver's license, unemployment insurance, and other services and benefits are conditional upon the development of these competencies. In our culture, these skills are developed through many institutions, including the family, the media, and the schools. Of course, it is the schools that are viewed as the principal delivery system for these skills, and, consequently, they have been given the most attention.

The role of the schools as instructors of basic skills is clearly defined in the actions of most state legislatures and in several significant judicial decisions. Neither have the federal government and courts been remiss in taking an active part in determining a national policy on language processes.

This growing legal framework of regulations, laws, and court decisions, shaping our beliefs, policies, and programs regarding reading and other language processes, has led to the active questioning of many of the assumptions, beliefs, and structures that underlie educational actions. This text compiles works raising such questions in order to provide information and to encourage the awareness of a very complex problem—that posed by the relationship between law and reading.

"Courts and Public Education," by Edward J. Schork and Stephen C. Miller, describes the origins of judicial activism in education. The intrusion of the courts into the educational process is seen as the last resort of a citizenry alarmed by the school system's apparent lack of response to educational problems. A review of past cases indicates two principles that may be used in court cases involving reading. These principles suggest that a child may not be excluded from a free education and that a child has a right to instruction appropriate to his or her individual needs. The problem confronting the courts and schools when these principles are applied to reading instruction and the possible ramifications of educational malpractice are also evaluated.

The decline in support for public education and in esteem for educators, reflected by the shift in responsibility for educational policy making, is discussed by Joan C. Baratz. This decline, brought about by many factors but primarily caused by great promises being made and little being accomplished, has resulted in a demand for quality with a focus on output, as measured by tests. A discussion of the consequences of this orientation focuses on two major policy issues: minimal literacy standards for graduation and funding based on test results. Baratz wonders whether minimal standards will turn into maximum standards and questions how schools have gotten themselves into this position. An examination of funding based on test scores raises many more questions, but, quite clearly, decisions in education are no longer entirely in the domain of the educator.

Nancy and Yehoash Dworkin discuss the concept of a provider/consumer relationship in the teaching of reading. This view of the future, should the trend in legislation and litigation continue, seems to pit the provider and consumer of educational services at loggerheads; provider and consumer disenchantment will continue as the courts become overloaded with educational malpractice suits. The authors encourage the establishment of a truly interactive system where all parties involved are accountable to and supportive of the reading program.

Robert E. Draba discusses the major issues involved in establishing reading as a graduation requirement, providing insight into specific legal considerations. He examines procedural due process in light of court decisions, as these decisions may have future bearing on similar challenges to the schools. A discussion of equal protection, school systems' classification methods (particularly as they regard the poor reader), and test bias indicates the need for a definitive procedure for detecting educational biases. The author concludes that a school system that believes it can deny students diplomas on the basis of reading ability and not have its classification method challenged is, at best, naive.

"What kind of reading will the law prescribe?" is a question that is being addressed as legislators and courts expand their influences in education. William D. Page discusses this question in terms of the necessity of defining reading. He analyzes three classes of reading definitions—iconic, analogical, and symbolic—and evaluates the usefulness and validity of each for establishing accountability. A discussion of the future role of the courts and the effects of court interventions suggests that the real solution to the problem of educational accountability lies in an emphasis on teacher education.

Daniel M. Schember recommends the enactment of new state statutes

requiring school districts to acquire, consider, and, where appropriate, implement research findings concerning promising instructional strategies. He
suggests that plans for the active consideration and deliberate selection of
alternate strategies for the teaching of reading are necessary. The need for
this legislation stems from both the continuing advances in the state of the
art of reading instruction and the imperatives of "right to education" litigation. He further suggests that the process of local decision making, to evaluate
current practices and to make changes, is hampered by thinking that seeks to
preserve the *status quo*. Indecision by the schools is unwarranted in light of
the current research findings and the expanding legal developments that will
most affect future schooling.

The final selection, by Robert J. Harper II and Gary Kilarr, suggests that
many of the basic assumptions about reading underlying the present relationship between law and reading may be incorrect or, at best, misinterpreted.
The lack of a common understanding and agreement has caused considerable
confusion and may, in fact, be diverting attention to inappropriate court
decisions, legislative activities, and educational practices. The emergence of a
new theory of reading instruction may be prohibited by these inappropriate
activities. Recognition that there is a problem is seen as the first step to
bringing clarity and resolution to the existing confusion.

Hopefully, with the insights provided by the various authors whose work
is collected here, the reader will continue the exploration that is necessary for
educators to achieve reasonable and just solutions. The final outcome of such
an exploration will encompass all aspects of the educational system.

# COURTS AND PUBLIC EDUCATION:
## Possibilities and Limits

EDWARD J. SCHORK
STEPHEN C. MILLER, ESQ.*

Public education and the courts have become increasingly intertwined during the last twenty years. The trend toward judicial activism in education started in 1954 with the seminal Supreme Court decision in *Brown* v. *Board of Education*. Since then, courts have ruled on educational issues ranging from a student's right to protest war to the fairness of financing schools with local taxes. School prayer, equal educational opportunity, curriculum, testing, exclusion, classification (by ability, race, or geography), and resource allocation are also among the significant educational issues which have been tried in the courtroom.[1]

Reactions to this intervention have been varied. Many observers consider court involvement an intrusion. Among them is University of Pennsylvania professor of education Bartell Cardon, who asserts, "It's an unfortunate thing that the courts are, in reality, telling educators how to educate."[2] Some judges also have reservations about the extent of court incursions into education. Oliver Gasch, of the United States District Court of the District of Columbia, maintains that judges lack the experience, training, and expertise to oversee the implementation of specific educational changes. He admonishes his colleagues, therefore, to "let the professionals run the schools."[3] Still others point out that basic societal issues are at stake in many cases and argue that legislatures and government agencies—not the courts—are the proper forum in which to decide social policy.[4]

On the other hand, the courts are seen as the last, or even only, resort by many groups. In particular, blacks and other minorities have resorted to the

*At the time of writing, Stephen C. Miller was director of and Edward J. Schork was research associate for the Philadelphia office of the Education Law Center, Inc.

courts to redress their grievances. In part, this is because other institutions have failed to respond to problems and vindicate and protect rights.[5]

In their role as the arbiters of justice, courts have the ability to craft remedies and create new forums to resolve problems. They also serve indirectly as an illuminating force, clarifying issues and articulating needs. This increases general awareness and directs the attention of decision makers, catalyzing educators and agencies who are directly responsible for the schools. However, the courts are not omnipotent.[6] As suggested above, courts have neither the time nor the expertise to be super-administrators of the schools. And many school systems are large organizations, with traits such as inertia, firmly held internal norms, and diffuse responsibility—characteristics which make them singularly resistant to change. Within such a system, failure to persuade teachers and principals of the value of a judicially mandated change may be sufficient to prevent its meaningful implementation.[7] Also, lack of specific guidelines and a special mechanism for implementation lessen the likelihood of compliance.[8] Finally, political realities dictate the limits of judicial authority, as, for example, in the *Robinson* v. *Cahill* crisis in New Jersey, where court-ordered changes in the method of funding public schools were stymied until legislators adopted new tax laws.

In general terms, then, what can court intervention accomplish in education? Kuriloff et al., studied legal reform and educational change in Pennsylvania. Their conclusions offer an apt summary:

> They can mandate substantive reform in general terms . . . they can bring into being procedural safeguards to assist in the implementation of safeguards to assist in the implementation of substantive reform . . . provide some supervision for the development and organization of implementation mechanisms . . . articulate in aspirational terms what is needed . . . give impetus to filling in the specific content of its general mandate.[9]

### Reading: The Problem and The Law

> A stable and democratic society is impossible without a minimum of literacy and knowledge on the part of most citizens . . . the gain from the education of a child accrues not only to the child or to his parents but also to other members of society.[10]

One area of education likely to receive considerable legal attention in the near future is that of essential skills, particularly reading skills. The ability to read is uniquely important, for upon it depends an individual's ability to obtain an education, to function effectively within and benefit from society, and to exercise political rights and responsibilities as a citizen.

In this light, the extent of illiteracy in America is particularly alarming. Illiteracy is defined in numerous ways, and indices of its prevalence vary accordingly, but a recent study of tests of functional adult literacy found that, "using several literacy tasks chosen simply as examples, the national level of marginal to complete illiteracy might encompass around ten percent of the population, and might be much higher among some minorities."[11] Another source reports that nearly 19 million Americans over age sixteen are functionally illiterate (here defined as unable to read at the fifth grade level)— a number equal to the populations of Los Angeles and New York City combined. Of the 51.5 million students who leave United States schools annually, an estimated 8 million, or 15 percent, cannot read. Every year, 70,000 students drop out of public school with reading skills lagging two or more years behind their grade level. The United States Office of Education supports a national Right to Read program which seeks to eliminate illiteracy by 1980; currently operating in all states, the program testifies to the importance and dimensions of the reading problem. Right to Read estimates that one out of four children in the nation has a serious reading disability.[12] These figures compellingly indicate that, for unacceptably many students, public education has been failing at one of its essential tasks.

While the challenge to educational institutions is clear, the courts are also likely to play a major role in reading education. Parents and concerned citizens, alarmed by statistics such as those above and encouraged by militant consumerism, are increasingly questioning the methods and performance of the schools. Many of the dissatisfied are expressing their grievances as legal challenges. Indeed, the courts have already been confronted with claims of "educational malpractice." Moreover, several cases have laid the foundation for future courtroom arguments regarding the nature of reading instruction and the circumstances under which a child may have legal rights to it.

*Reading in Court: Cases Past and Future*

Several recent cases suggest that a child has a right to an instructional program appropriate to his or her educational needs, and that students may not be excluded from free public education because of either organic or linguistic deficiencies. In *Pennsylvania Association for Retarded Children v. Commonwealth* (PARC), the parties involved entered into a consent decree which requires the state to provide "every retarded person . . . access to a free public program of education and training appropriate to his learning capacities."[13] Due process rights regarding classification and placement were also guaranteed.[14]

In a similar case, *Mills* v. *Board of Education*, the plaintiffs contested the failure of the District of Columbia public schools to provide education for exceptional children as well as challenged the schools' practice of excluding or transferring such children from regular classes without due process of law. As in Pennsylvania, the court found that the plaintiffs had been denied an equal educational opportunity and ordered that "a publicly supported education suited to his needs" be provided to each child of school age. The court also stated emphatically that "requiring parents to see that their children attend school under pain of criminal penalties presupposes that an educational opportunity will be made available to the children."[15]

In a third case, *Lau* v. *Nichols,* Chinese-speaking children argued that they receive little or no benefit from the regular public school program because of their limited ability to understand English—the language of instruction. In a unanimous decision, the United States Supreme Court concluded that "students who do not understand English are effectively foreclosed from any meaningful education."[16] The Court's decision resulted in the provision of remedial English instruction to enable these students to effectively participate in regular instruction. Again, the issues at stake were exclusion, in this case effective exclusion as a result of linguistic deficiency, and the nature of "meaningful educational opportunity" for students with special needs.

Taken together, these cases suggest several arguments that might be used in court cases involving reading. The key principles that emerge from them indicate first, that a child may not be excluded from a free public education; and second, that a child has a right to instruction appropriate to his or her individual educational needs.

On the basis of the first principle, it might be argued that reading deficiency, whether organic, social, or educational in origin, is a deficit similar to those of the handicapped children in *PARC* and *Mills* and the Chinese-speaking students in *Lau* in one important respect: inability to read impedes a child's overall learning to such an extent that he or she is, in the words of Justice Douglas, "effectively foreclosed from a meaningful education."[17] Thus, public school students who are seriously deficient in reading may be entitled to the amount of remedial reading instruction needed to enable them to benefit from the regular curriculum. However, this argument depends upon the ability of educators to answer a number of difficult questions: What is reading ability? What aspects of it can be reliably measured? and, What performance on a reading test corresponds to the ability to benefit from a normal instructional program? How much reading instruction, and what kind of instruction, is needed to bring individual students to the point where they are no longer effectively excluded?

It is unclear whether these questions can be answered in terms sufficiently unambiguous to persuade a court. There is no consensus regarding the optimal methods by which to teach reading, and a recent comprehensive critique of reading tests indicates that test effectiveness is hampered by numerous problems of design, by statistical fallacies, and by limitations upon their valid use.[18]

The second principle, that which ensures an "appropriate education," suggests two conclusions regarding reading. First, a right to appropriate education would mean that, for a student who is deficient in reading, the instructional program must be directed at remedying his or her reading problem. This argument assumes that it is an educational need of the deficient reader to read at a normal level, regardless of how severe his or her deficiency may be. This interpretation thus requires the remediation of all reading deficiencies, not just those that are so severe as to, in effect, exclude students from the curriculum's benefits. In so doing, this principle reflects the same goal as the argument regarding exclusion, but would demand a remedy for more students.

An alternative interpretation of the concept of "appropriate education" is broader still, extending to all students, whether reading-deficient, "normal," or "gifted." It simply asserts that all children are entitled to individualized reading instruction because only instruction that is directed toward their current level of reading ability is appropriate to their educational needs. The breadth of this argument makes it attractive; however, it may also prove to be a handicap. Individualized instruction in reading would be ideal—for reading development. But schools have limited resources, and the cost of implementing individualized reading instruction for all students would be, at the least, formidable. Thus, demands for this type of program, or even the less extensive remedial programs referred to above, raise a thorny question: Should progress in reading ability be stressed even at the risk of less learning in other areas? In distributing limited resources, schools must balance the special needs of some students—for example, the needs of the reading deficient for remedial instruction—with their responsibility to provide the best possible education to all students, normal and gifted, as well as handicapped and deficient. As educator Jerome Bruner has observed, "There are also requirements for productivity to be met: are we producing enough scholars, scientists, poets, lawmakers, to meet the demands of our times?"[19]

The courts are reluctant to make such quintessentially educational decisions or to impose large, costly programs on overburdened school districts. For this reason, while the foregoing arguments for remedial and individualized reading instruction may be made on the basis of the cases cited, how the courts will respond to suits that seek sweeping changes in reading education cannot be predicted.

To date, court activity in education has dealt primarily with equality of educational opportunity and resource distribution. The cases discussed above, while fundamentally concerned with equal protection, begin to focus upon the substance of education by introducing the question, What constitutes an appropriate program of instruction? A recent case goes right to the heart of educational practice by bringing the nature and equality of educational services provided by the public schools under judicial scrutiny and by questioning whether there is a professional standard against which services can be measured.

In *Peter Doe* v. *San Francisco Unified School District*, a high school graduate claimed that school personnel were to blame for his functional illiteracy.[20] Although Peter's IQ, attendance, grades, and reported reading ability had been average during his twelve years in the San Francisco schools, he could only read at a fifth-grade level at the time of his graduation. Peter sued the school system for a million dollars in damages as compensation for his injuries—nonlearning. Specifically, his complaint alleged that the school district was liable for negligence, misrepresentation, and breach of duties by acts and omissions involving not only instruction, but also guidance, counseling, supervision, evaluation, promotion, and reports of ability and progress. The California Superior Court dismissed Doe's complaint, and the case was appealed to an intermediate state court of appeals, where the decision was given in favor of the school district. Other such cases are pending in both New York and Pennsylvania.

Proponents of "educational malpractice" lawsuits such as Peter's argue that compensation should be available for individual plaintiffs and that the threat of damages will provide the schools with an incentive to increase efficiency and decrease the number of nonlearners.[21] University of California at Berkeley law professor Stephen Sugarman observes that school children and their parents have only limited power in their role as consumers of education. He concludes that individual lawsuits for damages are, therefore, a more promising avenue for educational reform than lobbying and other "Nader-style" attempts to induce educational change. Critics of this approach point out, however, that damages would probably be paid from a school system's general budget, which would reduce the level of funds available for instructional expenditures and would, therefore, produce more, not fewer, nonlearners.[22]

The *Doe* case has been characterized as an attempt to achieve educational accountability through the courts.[23] It poses a number of exceedingly difficult questions for judges and educators: How can a court specify complex standards for learning when educators themselves are far from unanimous in their specification of goals and appraisal of various programs and methods? Who in public education will be ultimately responsible for meeting these standards?[24] and, What yardstick will be used to determine whether these standards are being met? Indeed, these questions may prove so formidable that courts will decline to hear educational malpractice cases such as *Doe* on the grounds that they lack competence or that there is insufficient knowledge about learning and teaching to reliably evaluate the complicated issues involved. The courts may also conclude that they lack jurisdiction.[25] Should they be willing to decide, however, they must also specify appropriate remedies, which may likewise prove difficult.[26] If damages are to be paid, it is unclear what price should be put upon intangible injuries such as loss in earning capacity or pain and suffering. Reimbursement for tutoring is an obvious remedy, but one which is complicated by the need for yet another educational standard: that which can define the level of ability the plaintiff is entitled to achieve through tutoring. Compensation might also be paid for wages lost during tutoring, but this would entail determining the salary level of someone who has not yet worked. The value of more free schooling in the system which has already failed the student seems questionable; a court might, therefore, provide for additional instruction in a private school. Judges must also decide whether they will seek to prevent future failures by sanctioning teachers or school officials or by ordering programatic changes. Finally, what recourse will be allowed to schools regarding children who cannot achieve minimum proficiency? Withholding the diploma or awarding a lesser certificate are likely alternatives.

What is likely to result from a favorable decision in a case such as that of Peter Doe? While this cannot be predicted with certainty, several interesting possibilities exist. Schools might seek to improve counseling and communication with parents regarding student progress.[27] Higher standards for the hiring and evaluation of school personnel might also result. As a means to this end, schools may establish distinct categories for teachers with different qualifications, responsibilities, and pay scales.[28] Ultimately, individual school sites may be evaluated and held accountable as units, based on annual reports which each school files concerning pupil performance and overall school progress.[29]

A favorable decision in *Doe*, and increased demands for accountability in general, may also have a negative impact upon education in several ways. If performance on reading tests is heavily stressed, reading instructors may teach only those skills which the tests measure. Since reading tests measure word-recognition and decoding skills more effectively than the ability to transform a decoded message into meaning, the teaching of reading comprehension may be neglected.[30] Or, worse yet, reading instruction may degenerate into "test training," which amounts to teaching the test rather than teaching reading. This method of "instruction" artificially inflates reading test scores but does not improve reading ability.[31] *Doe* might also result in an overemphasis upon basic skills at the expense of other kinds of learning. While basic competencies are clearly essential, the acquisition of certain knowledge and values is likewise a central goal of education.[32] Finally, parents of struggling students may be increasingly tempted to blame the schools for their children's difficulties, requiring schools to expend exorbitant amounts of energy in defense of educational failures.

Further legal attempts to hold schools accountable are likely to focus upon the establishment of more rigorous certification procedures and more comprehensive on-the-job assessment of teachers and other staff. From a practical viewpoint, it is more desirable to set accountability standards for personnel performance than for pupil performance, as the amount of testing needed to evaluate student achievement in all subjects would be prohibitive. However, regular evaluation of each student's proficiency in the basic skills is feasible, and cases which emphasize the schools' duties to students in reading and other fundamentals are the most probable sequel to *Doe.*

*Conclusion*

Former Secretary of the Department of Health, Education and Welfare John Gardner once remarked that "our kind of society demands the maximum development of individual potentialities at every level of ability."[33] There is no question that the schools are expected to perform this function. It remains to be seen, however, whether they will do so alone or under the impetus of court intervention.

## Notes

1. For an overview of court actions on educational issues, see M. McGann Steege, "Courts and Classrooms," *Pennsylvania Gazette* 74 (1976) 28-31; and Donna E. Shalala and James A. Kelly, "Politics, the Courts and Educational Policy," *Teachers' College Record* 75 (1973): 223-37.

2. As quoted in Steege, "Courts and Classrooms," p. 28.

3. Gasch, "Education, Society, and the Law," *NASSP Bulletin* 60 (1976): 6-11.

4. For example, University of Pennsylvania law professor Stephen Goldstein. In Steege, "Courts and Classrooms," p. 29.

5. In an address delivered at the National Conference on the Causes of Popular Dissatisfaction with the Administration of Justice, Judge Leon A. Higgenbotham, Jr., of the United States District Court, stated: "A basic reason for the necessity of having the courts available to vindicate the rights of citizens is that other institutions in our society designed to vindicate or protect those rights have either failed to do so or have broken down completely." (70 F.R.D. 79, 155, April 7-9, 1976).

6. See Peter Kuriloff et al., "Legal Reform and Educational Change: The Pennsylvania Case," *Exceptional Children* 41 (1974): 41.

7. See Dale Mann, "Making Change Happen?" *Teachers' College Record* 77 (1967): 313-22; Richard L. Mandel, "Judicial Decisions and Organizational Change in Public Schools," *School Review* (1974): 327-46; and Larry Cuban, "*Hobson* v. *Hansen:* A Study in Organizational Response," *Educational Administration Quarterly* 11 (1975): 15-37.

8. Kuriloff, "Legal Reform."

9. *Ibid.*

10. Milton Friedman, *Capitalism and Freedom* (Chicago: University of Chicago Press, 1962), p. 85.

11. Dean H. Nafziger et al., *Tests of Functional Adult Literacy*, (Portland, Ore.: Northwest Regional Educational Laboratory, 1975), p. 17. [ED 109 265]

12. This statistic and those preceding it are reported in Ralph D. Berenger, "The Ambitious Goal of Right to Read," *Compact* 9 (1975): 2-5.

13. 334 F. Supp. 1257 (E.D. Pa. 1971); and 343 F. Supp 279 (E.D. Pa. 1972).

14. In a consent decree settling a subsequent case, *Catherine D.* v. *Pittenger* (Civil No. 74-2435, E.D. Pa. 1974), both the right to "appropriate education" and the due process protections of the *PARC* decree were extended by the Pennsylvania State Board of Education to every exceptional child in Pennsylvania, including "normal" and "gifted" children.

15. *Mills* v. *Board of Education*, 348 F. Supp. 866 (D.D.C. 1972).

16. *Lau* v. *Nichols*, 414 U.S. 563 (1974). For a discussion of *PARC*, *Mills*, and *Lau*, see David Kirp and Mark Yudoff, *Educational Policy and the Law* (Berkeley, Cal.: McCutchan,

1974); Robert E. Lindquist and Arthur E. Wise, "Developments in Education Litigation: Equal Protection, *"Journal of Law and Education* 5 (1976): 46-55; and Stephen R. Goldstein, *Law and Public Education* (New York: Bobbs-Merril Co., Inc., 1974).

17. *Lau* v. *Nichols.*

18. Kenneth S. Goodman, "Testing in Reading: A General Critique," in Robert B. Ruddell, ed., *Accountability in Reading Instruction: Critical Issues* (Urbana, Ill.: National Council of Teachers of English, 1973), pp. 21-33. [ED 073 448]

19. *The Process of Education* (New York: Vintage Books, 1960), p. 9.

20. Civil No. 36851 1st District Ct. App. (1975).

21. For a discussion of pertinent legal theories, see Stephen D. Sugarman, "Accountability through the Courts," *School Review* 82 (1974): 233-259, and "Educational Malpractice," *University of Pennsylvania Law Review* 124 (1976): 755-805.

22. Sugarman, "Accountability," pp. 227, 234.

23. *Ibid.*

24. Gary Saretsky, "The Strangely Significant Case of Peter Doe," *Phi Delta Kappan* 14 (1973): 589.

25. See *Scheelhaase* v. *Woodbury Central Community School District*, 349 F. Supp. 988, (D. Iowa 1972), *rev'd.*, 488 R.2d 237 (8th Cir. 1973), *cert denied*, 94 S. Ct. 3173 (1974), a case brought by a teacher who had been terminated by her school district due to incompetence, as allegedly indicated by her pupils' achievement test scores. The 8th Circuit Court of Appeals dismissed the case because "such matters as the competence of teachers, and the standards of its measurement are not, without more, matters of constitutional dimension."

26. For a discussion of damage awards in educational malpractice suits, see Sugarman, "Accountability," pp. 250-53.

27. Sugarman, "Accountability," p. 246.

28. See James W. Guthrie, "Public Control of Public Schools—What Can We Do to Restore It?," *PSBA Bulletin* 39 (1975): 11.

29. Guthrie, "Public Control, " p. 10. In a recent case, *Chappell* v. *Commissioner of Education of New Jersey*, 135 N.J. Super. 565, 343 A. 2d 811 (1975), the court affirmed a decision by the State Board of Education to disseminate the results of statewide achievement tests in reading and mathematics, as well as interpretive materials, and stated that "information provided by these 'interpreted' reports will be helpful . . . in the allocation of resources, in shaping educational goals, in focusing on the improvement of basic skills, and in shedding light on the functioning of the public schools."

30. Goodman, "Testing in Reading," p. 32. See also Richard E. Hodges, "Some Assumptions about Behavioral Objectives," in *Accountability and Reading Instruction*, p. 18.

31. Pierre de Vise, "Chicago's Improved Reading Scores," *Integrated Education* 14 (1976): 13.

32. Hodges, "Assumptions about Behavioral Objectives," p. 14.

33. *No Easy Victories* (New York: Harper & Row, Publishers, 1968), p. 65.

# POLICY ISSUES IN EDUCATION:
# Reading and the Law

JOAN C. BARATZ*

In the past decade, there has been a decline in support for public education and in esteem for school officials. This has been apparent in several ways: not only have public opinion polls indicated a drop in confidence regarding the educational system's ability to satisfactorily instruct the children for whom it is responsible, but taxpayers have refused again and again to vote for bond issues or to raise taxes in support of local education. Another manifestation of these declines is the growing tension between professional educators and administrators, and those public officials charged with setting educational policy—school board members, legislators, and, more recently, judges. Whereas ten years ago it was commonplace for school superintendents to submit their policies to school boards and have them "ratified" in a *pro forma* manner, in the last few years, school board members, especially those in urban areas, have attempted to assert their authority by questioning superintendents' decisions and by developing their own educational strategies. The result has been protracted battle between boards and superintendents, with a high rate of turn-over for superintendents of large school districts.

This shift in policy making responsibility from almost exclusive control by the educational community has also been reflected in the growing involvement of judges in the creation of educational policy. As frustration with the school establishment as an arbitrator of grievances grows, citizens have turned to the courts for answers. Courts have had to deal with such diverse educational issues as school punishment procedures, desegregation, educational

*Joan C. Baratz is director of the Educational Policy Research Institute of the Educational Testing Service, Washington, D.C.

services for the handicapped, equalization of school resources, setting educational standards, and claims of "educational malpractice." These latter two issues are central to the definition of the relationship between law and reading. While desegregation and school finance issues have tended to treat information concerning academic performance as somewhat peripheral to the legal issues concerned, cases involving educational standards (such as *Robinson* v. *Cahill* in New Jersey)[1] and malpractice (as reflected in *Peter Doe* v. *San Francisco*)[2] have tended to bring the question of reading performance to the fore.

In the '60s and early '70s, the educational policies that occupied both the courts and legislatures were generally concerned with equity. Reflecting the militancy of the '60s and the concern that tests unfairly categorized minority-group individuals, many professionals viewed performances on standardized tests as suspect. In fact, a series of cases attempted to establish the discriminatory nature of such tests.[3] Concern generally centered on issues of equal distribution of educational services.

With the Nixon administration came a systems-analysis approach, a growing conservatism, and a disillusionment with the gap between what the "Great Society" had promised and what it had achieved. Money was tight, and attention began to focus on the results of educational programs. The question of competency in basic skills became central. Studies about grade inflation and the decline in Scholastic Aptitude Test scores began to be given wide circulation in the media. The business community gave voice to its concerns about the unemployability of a large portion of our high school youth. *Quality*, rather than *equality* had become the watchword of discussions of education.

This focus on output, as measured by test scores (especially those reflecting basic skill competencies), has raised two major questions: Should minimal standards of literacy be established for graduation, and Should funding be based on test scores? Both these questions involve a series of policy issues that must be examined in greater detail.

## The Setting of Minimal Standards

Recently, concerns have been expressed for the adequacy of graduating high school students' reading and mathematics skills, and the "functional literacy" of these students has also been called into question. These concerns have led to proposals that require students to demonstrate competencies in basic skills in order to receive their diplomas. Kern County, California will withhold diplomas this year from students who do not demonstrate certain levels of proficiency in reading and math; Arizona requires students to be able to read, write, and compute at the ninth-grade level; the Los Angeles, California, city school system has developed the Senior High Achievement and Reading Proficiency Test, a measure involving ten subskills that all students must master for graduation in 1978; Oregon has mandated that, by 1978, every local district must develop minimum competency standards for graduation; and, in 1979, New York City will require all high school students to demonstrate mastery of reading and mathematics at the ninth-grade level. Similar type bills are pending in Kansas, Tennessee, Virginia, Pennsylvania, Georgia, and Maryland state houses.[4]

In addition to laws passed at the state level, many local jurisdictions are passing resolutions requiring demonstration of competencies for graduation. In New Jersey, the issue is being debated in the courtroom: the setting of state minimal standards has been requested by some parties to the *Robinson* v. *Cahill* suit as a demonstration of the state's obligation to provide a "thorough and efficient" education that will allow each student to participate in the labor market and perform his or her duties as a citizen.

The New Jersey court case debate concerns not just graduation standards, but minimum standards at various grade levels. This is also the case in Florida, where the state legislature has enacted a law that calls for minimum standards to be set by 1977 for promotion from elementary schools as well as from high schools. California currently has a bill in the legislature that also requires the demonstration of competencies for promotion. Other states are beginning to debate the practice of requiring students to demonstrate established levels of proficiency, and the following questions are being addressed:

1. What is the obligation of the state toward students who reach graduation age and cannot pass the tests?
2. What is the relationship between such testing and equal educational opportunity, particularly if such tests are shown to adversely affect the options of minority group students?
3. What constitutes a minimum level of literacy for functioning in the "real world?" Do tests exist that can assess such competency?
4. Is it justifiable to withhold a diploma in, for example, New York City for failure to display ninth-grade competency when, in another jurisdiction, only eighth-grade competency is required?
5. If promotion is based on competency, what is to be done with students who are unable to pass elementary proficiency exams?
6. Will minimum standards turn into maximum standards?
7. Who will bear the anticipated cost of remedial education for students who do not pass these tests?
8. What eventually happens to students who do not succeed in passing the tests?

These policy issues have direct impact for reading specialists. It is the reading teacher, not the policy maker, who will ultimately be called upon to both define and defend the minimal standards. The laws, however, do not specify criteria for reading, they merely call for the establishment of minimal competency levels. Not only will reading specialists be pressed for a professional certification of functional reading, they will also have to be prepared to develop reading programs that will ensure that students who initially fail the minimal competency tests are given appropriate instruction.

The imposition of these laws has direct implications for the reading profession as well. It will have to confront such questions as: What is "functional literacy?" How shall functional literacy be assessed and taught? and, Is functional literacy different from reading competency?

Another policy issue closely related to the imposition of minimum standards concerns high school equivalency diplomas. The California legislature, in an effort to make high schools more responsive to the needs of students, has passed a law requiring the state department of education to develop a test to serve as an alternative means of achieving a high school diploma. The California High School Proficiency Examination, which students sixteen years or older can take to receive a certificate of equivalency, was the result of this mandate. The test was developed by using items from tests such as the Texas Adult Literacy Test and from a minimum proficiency test developed by Murphy at the Educational Testing Service;[5] items developed by officials within the California Department of Education were incorporated as well. Passing the test is not only a certification of proficiency, but allows students to finish high school earlier. Other states are indicating interest in the implementation of high school equivalency examinations. Questions of policy deriving from this development include the following: Who takes these tests? What happens to students who are able to exit early from high school? and, Since most high schools receive monies based on average daily attendance, and this test allows some students to leave during the school year, what possible effects on funding may be anticipated?

### Test-based Funding

In 1965, the landmark Elementary and Secondary Education Act's (ESEA) Title I provision focused on assisting students with educational problems. Identifying students who would be eligible for the extra funds provided by Title I involved, among other things, criteria related to students' family income. It has long been recognized that children from poverty homes exhibit many educational problems and that additional funds may be necessary in order to provide these youngsters with an equal educational opportunity. In recent years, where there has been an emphasis on school finance reform, state laws have been passed that, either through categorical grants or through pupil weighting systems, have provided extra resources to schools with a large number of youngsters from poverty families.

Recently, there has been increased discussion about providing funds to schools not on the basis of poverty indices, but on the basis of test scores. While the renewal of the ESEA act was being debated, Congressman Quie, a Republican from Minnesota, introduced an amendment that would make the allotment of Title I funds contingent upon test results demonstrating educational disadvantagement, regardless of the socioeconomic background of the student in question. While the amendment was defeated, it did not resolve the issue of test-based funding at the state and local levels.

Additional policy issues derive from the use of test scores as a criterion for the allocation of resources. Addressing the following questions may help to define the impact of test-based funding:

1. Will schools tend to depress scores to secure more funds? Is testing an incentive for educational systems to do poorly?
2. Will there be a tendency to inflate scores to avoid the consequences of being labeled a school or class of nonlearners?
3. What will happen to schools whose test scores increase after an influx of funds? Will they lose such funds when scores improve?
4. Will money be siphoned off from the poorer schools to assist more affluent students?
5. Will the subject matter evaluated by the tests used for allocating funds preempt other important skills that the school is responsible for teaching?

While the issues surrounding debates on reading are complex, decisions relating to them affect teachers and students alike. One thing seems clear: those decisions are no longer likely to be made solely by reading researchers or other educational experts.

## Notes

1. 62 N.J. 473 (1973).

2. Civil No. 36851 1st District Ct. App. (1975).

3. For example, *Lau* v. *Nichols*, 414 U.S. 563 (1974); and *Larry P.* v. *Riles*, 343 F. Supp. 1306 (1972).

4. J. Baratz and S. Thant, *Test Data and Politics: A Survey of State Test Policy Uses* (Washington, D.C.: Educational Policy Research Institute, 1978).

5. See Ellen Polgar, "The California High School Proficiency Exam" (Ph.D. diss., University of California at Berkeley, 1976). [ED 129 859]

# A PROVIDER/CONSUMER RELATIONSHIP BETWEEN READING PROFESSIONALS AND THE PUBLIC

NANCY E. DWORKIN
YEHOASH S. DWORKIN*

Over the past decade, there has been a marked change in the relationship between the school establishment and the public, a change culminating in "consumer oriented" legislation. Both Public Law 94–142, which states generally that all children are entitled to an equal education in a form which deviates least from the traditional educational environment, and federal and state accountability laws represent a departure from the classical perspective of interaction between educator and learner, which viewed the former as the professional decision maker and the latter as the recipient of services.[1] Indeed, contemporary social attitudes, as well as legal structures, have moved citizens and educators into advocacy positions, and significant implications exist for the school professional with regard to legal liability and legitimate provision of educational services.

While the issues discussed here derive specifically from various aspects of accountability, one cannot escape the impact of Public Law 94–142 as a specific factor in determining future educational trends. It is clear that the law has moved in the direction of asserting what we might term "consumer rights." Both parent and child have been accorded a role in educational decision making which has traditionally been viewed as the preserve of the professional educator.[2] The consequences of such consumer involvement become most critical in relation to educational planning and participation in the diagnostic process. Thus, where accountability schema are developed, it

*Nancy E. Dworkin is director of the Center for Unique Learners, Information and Service Modules, Inc., Maryland. Yehoash S. Dworkin is director of research and evaluation for Information and Service Modules, Inc.

becomes necessary to include input from individuals who, heretofore, would have been viewed as only recipients.

Aside from the ethical imperatives established by such a partnership, we are confronted with a series of critical challenges to the traditional operating procedures of school professionals, including reading specialists and other educational experts. While it should be stated at the outset that current federal legislation does not hold such specialists individually responsible,[3] and that most state and local formulae concentrate primarily on the accountability of classroom teachers, there is little question that area specialists will be answerable within the accountability mandates of the school system.[4] Furthermore, unless the current climate undergoes drastic change, it can be assumed that specialists, as their roles as educational providers are clarified, will increasingly be included in accountability formulae. According to Public Law 94-142, they are already identified as potential participants in diagnostic teams, and where planning calls for the utilization of specialists, they are further identified by name and function.

It is clear that any form of accountability, in order to be viable, must be related to an established and measurable set of criteria. In addition, those criteria must be open to standardization, at least within individual school systems. There is no possibility of developing an acceptable balance between responsibility and liability where measures vary from school to school, district to district, and so on. Given the necessity for such evaluation, therefore, it is evident that measures of reading must occupy a major role in legal and formal assessment.

Although issues such as test validity, performance and behavioral objectives, short-term versus long-term educational gains, culture bias, and other factors are currently prominent, it is clear that reading does now, and will continue to, serve as a major measure of school success.[5] Consumers, legislators, and providers all agree that progress through the school system cannot be separated from progress in reading development. While such thinking is certainly not new, the relationship between reading progress and the general system of accountability has highlighted a number of issues for future concern.

### Changing Relationships

The immediate effect of legislating accountability is to change the relationships between school professionals, including specialists, and the general citizenry and between educators and their professional groups. Classically, accountability for professionals has been established by creating standards and criteria for certification and by defining inservice commitments that are subject to internal review. According to this schema, it is assumed that professional competency can be validated through specific certification of teaching skills, skills based on operational standards deemed necessary for carrying out the obligations of the field. Further, most professional groups require some commitment, formal or informal, as part of the certification procedure. Protection of the recipient of services is also implied by demanding that the providers of service be evaluated by their professional peers. The inservice violations of teachers, therefore, have been viewed as relative to the commitments of the profession and have been judged by the same groups responsible for delineating appropriate punitive action.[6] Exceptions to the peer-group evaluation mechanism have occurred where professional violations also involved legal transgressions. (This practice is also illustrated in as high an office as the presidency, where only violations of law are open to judicial review and all other acts are subject only to internal peer review.)

The moment that professional accountability is related to legislative acts, the structure of internal peer review is subjected to substantial change, with a concommitent realignment of relationships. No longer is the individual practitioner answerable exclusively to the certification agent. Professional relationships must therefore be balanced against external responsibilities. More critically, the relationship between the provider of professional services and the recipient of those services undergoes marked reorganization. In effect, the professional enters into a provider/consumer relationship in which the rights and desires of the buyer become as critical as professional standards of performance.[7]

Clearly, these changed relationships are a mixed blessing. On the one hand, one can hardly argue the legitimacy of professional responsiveness to consumer interests. On the other hand, there is the dual danger that the consumer is neither sufficiently expert in specific areas to insist on viable standards, nor sufficiently directed to discriminate political, social, economic, and other influences which might be totally unrelated to the expertise required of the professional.

For the reading professional, such a change in status is extremely important. Not only does the individual reading specialist fall within the general accountability structure established by his or her local school system, but the area of reading itself serves as a measure of school-system efficacy. Almost every state which has dealt with accountability measures has included reading as a major criterion for program evaluation. As a result, school professionals in areas other than reading are held accountable for reading measures when their work in any way reflects written language. In consequence, the training generally reserved for reading professionals has been made available to school practitioners whose interests may be only tangential to reading, but whose responsibilities now require concern for reading measures.

Clearly, a mixed blessing: for many reading specialists, the utopian dream has been to make theories of reading and reading development available to all who deal with the delivery of information to children. From this vantage point, educational accountability has served as the catalytic agent in implementing such training. The rigorous standards painstakingly developed by major reading agencies such as the International Reading Association are, however, difficult to apply where reading courses are simply added to the general training of teachers. In short, accountability has not only changed the professional and provider/consumer relationships for reading specialists, but it has also created a new relationship between the specialty of reading and other teaching disciplines. As a final note, since accountability measures have led to the offering of reading courses to a general professional audience, it is reasonable to assume that institutions of higher learning will have to reassess reading-course content in terms ot its appropriateness for school practitioners whose objectives are substantially different than those of reading specialists.

## Changing Responsibilities and Liabilities

The introduction of a consumer relationship implies a serious reformulation of professional rights and obligations, especially as they relate to issues of legitimate practice, reward, and liability. The development of a legal accountability schema carries with it provisions for legal liability and redress in the face of violation. Clearly, no accountability procedure is meaningful unless the system spells out the penalties involved for substandard performance or malpractice. Admittedly, throughout most of the country, the reading professional is one step removed from the liability issue, since the major accountability formulae apply specifically to classroom teachers and the general school administration. Nevertheless, where accountability measures recognize the right of the individual consumer to petition for redress, it is potentially possible for any school professional to be directly and personally involved in the judicial machinery.

Once again, accountability brings with it a mixed blessing and some unique problems for the reading specialist. Certainly, it is a virtue for society to be concerned enough for its learners to demand that those who teach and those who function within the teaching environment be made responsible for the legitimacy of the services they provide. In other words, safeguards against malpractice constitute a major consumer right. A problem, however, arises the moment we shift focus from the actual provision of professional services to progress on the part of the recipient. In the provision of services, professional responsibility is confined to the arena where the professional has control, namely in the areas of training, diagnosis, individualized planning, and delivery of services. Where the progress of the recipient forms the basis for evaluation, there is the danger of making providers responsible for recipients' improper use of services. An analogous case might be where one makes the physician responsible for the patient's misuse of medication, where the patient has been appropriately briefed on proper procedures for its administration. Even in the most severe malpractice suits, the judicial system does not demand that the physician be responsible for the behavior of his or her parients; accountability only extends to the selection of legitimate procedures, the development of reasonable safeguards, and clear communication with the patient regarding these two issues.

Within the school structure, current legislation challenges two privileges traditionally maintained by educators: first, the educator's confinement of responsibility to the physical school environment, and second, the educator's prerogative to make services available only to those individuals who, in his or her best judgment, are capable of benefit. There is no question that these controls hold the potential for abuse, especially the latter, through which practitioners can "clear the classroom" of those children whose behaviors or learning styles do not meet their personal standards. Redress of such abuse, however, should not demand responsibility that cannot be associated with direct input. A child's progress is dependent on many factors in addition to appropriate school services; the problem in defining accountability relates to the offer of redress in cases where the abuse may lie with the consumer. Can a teacher sue a parent whose child is habitually late to class? Can a reading specialist "dismiss" a child who fails to do his or her homework? Can working professionals withdraw where space, time, and materials as well as administrative and legislative changes impinge upon the agreed upon remediation? In short, does accountability assume a closed-loop relationship between all the principal individuals in the child's educational environment, or is the flow of liability and redress a unidirectional one? While it is fair to make a reading specialist accountable for test selection, diagnostic precision, the development of reasonable objectives, and the delivery of teaching systems, it is not safe to assume that these will automatically result in progress on the part of the child, unless the school environment is the child's total environment. While "the popular view that teachers oppose the principle of accountability. . . . is . . . more myth than fact,"[8] the distribution of liability still remains a factor in evaluating the equity of new legislation.

If the above were simply a question of professional rights versus children's rights, these authors' votes would be in favor of the learners. The problem, however, is more complex than that of simple confrontation between provider and consumer. When large systems perceive a danger from external sources, they tend to become self-protective. As a result, the attempt to define accountability in areas in which the system has no input can become counterproductive. Certainly one can easily envision a system which directs its attention primarily toward those measures by which individuals will be judged. If reading achievement is measured against scores derived from test items, then that achievement in turn identifies reading progress, and it becomes safe to assume that many teachers and reading specialists will focus their instruction upon the test items or upon test taking itself. Indeed, one would have to defend the logic of a different course of action, since most systems draw a direct parallel between specific, measurable objectives and system operations.

Even more critical, however, is the danger of consumer exclusion from the decision-making process. Much of the thrust of accountability legislation and of Public Law 94–142 is directed toward the inclusion of consumers in the various operations of the school system. Prominent in such legislation is the role of the parent. Part of the intent of this action has been to move the parent from passive acceptance of professional input to active involvement in the planning, as well as the execution, of teaching objectives. When accountability, however, is unilaterally directed towards school professionals and without parallel legal responsibility on the part of the parents, there is the danger that practitioners will resist input counter to their own sense of professional validity. If the professional is made totally responsible for carrying out specific educational plans, it is highly probable that he or she will resist input from outside the purview of professional control and reject programs that reach beyond assumed achievable limits. Thus, two of the concerns of accountability legislation, the provision of educational service to every child and the inclusion of parents at every level of diagnosis and planning (which the authors believe to be critical for effective school operations), may come under attack when output, rather than process, becomes the standard for liability decisions.[9] If professionals are held accountable for behaviors and actions outside their control and are affected by planning input which is not subject to professional validation or certification, they may be forced to assume a counterproductive stance. Professionals who are held accountable for appropriate professional selections and delivery, however, might be encouraged to include input from parents and children, since such information leads to greater precision and legitimacy of choice.

*Liability versus Rights*

One of the problems in assessing the impact of current legislation and in evaluating the literature on current legislation is the frequent confusion between the protection of rights and the imposition of liability. The two are not necessarily related to each other in a symbiotic manner, and the problem posed for the school professional is to determine whether accountability legislation and its concomitant judicial liability structure may not, in the long run, seriously damage the protection of both consumer and provider rights.

In the case of protecting consumer rights, Public Law 94–142 has, in effect, made explicit the right of every child to an education most appropriate to that child's condition and least restricting to that child's functioning within the standard school environment. In a real sense, the complex of legislative acts posits a "mini-max" problem, stating, in effect, that every child is entitled to maximum education with minimal infringement upon the most commonly accepted form of school delivery system: the traditional classroom. As a result, all planning must take into account the fact that the school system may no longer withhold services on the basis of a child's assumed inability to function within a given educational setting. Rather, the system is obligated to start from the premise that every child is potentially teachable— any incursion or diminution of standard delivery systems must be fully documented and defended in terms of professional judgments and procedures.

Furthermore, parents' rights also are clearly delineated, especially as they refer to participation at three critical levels: first, during the diagnostic stage, where it is accepted that parental knowledge of the child's past and present history constitute an invaluable resource; second, in the planning process, where it is assumed that personal concern for the child will act to balance professionals' more abstract conceptions; and third, in the delivery process, which cannot be initiated without parental consent.

The general thrust of Public Law 94–142, then, makes explicit to the specialist the right of the nonprofessional to participate where his or her most intimate family interests are at stake. Aside from the legal implications, one cannot help but be impressed by the direction that legislation has taken, stating, in effect, that professionally trained practitioners can benefit from the insights of the primary agents in the child's life: the child's parents.

For the reading professional, however, such legislation presents a unique problem. Current statistics on adult illiteracy, whether defined functionally or absolutely, indicate that a high percentage of American adults have not fully mastered the skills and techniques of reading. Nevertheless, the rights of parents to participate in diagnostic and planning sessions make it possible for them to exert control over their children's reading programs. Hopefully, reading professionals will solve this problem by acting as a resource for parents, as well as for children and the general school system. Clearly, parents' comfort within the school setting and the ultimate value of parental input will be substantially enhanced if reading professionals also help parents develop reading and coping skills.

If Public Law 94–142 most clearly exemplifies the position of rights, accountability legislation most clearly exemplifies the position of liability. The fundamental assumption of accountability legislation is that protection is most directly achieved by assigning liability to violations of appropriate practice. Thus, where legislation dealing with rights emphasizes interaction between provider and consumer, accountability legislation emphasizes the criteria by which systems may be judged to have carried out their educational functions and defines the potential redress available to those parties who have suffered real or assumed damages.[10]

*A Statement of Advocacy*

There is no question that accountability legislation represents a response, on the part of responsible political and educational authorities, to many of the ills of our massive school systems. The general implications of such legislation reflect a greater concern for the rights of consumer populations, whether parents or children; increased sensitivity to the parent's role in decision making concerning the child's educational future; the establishment of standards and measurement criteria by which school systems and educators may be held accountable to the public; and the exploration of behavioral, as well as performance, criteria through which individual planning may take place.

One may assume that any legislation aimed at redressing prior problems can represent both threat and challenge to established systems. Accountability legislation is no exception. Compounding problems are the issues that are emphasized in the popular, and even some of the professional, literature. A great deal of attention has been paid to the possible impact of accountability measures on job retention and promotion. Furthermore, the lack of standardization of evaluation criteria from state to state and theoretical problems in some of the test measures currently in use give educators and evaluators cause for concern. In a real sense, part of the problem stems not from the content of specific state and federal acts, but from the decades of suspicion and mistrust which have developed between school systems and citizens. Perhaps, in order to effect dramatic changes, it is necessary to pass through a period of experimentation.

From the point of view of this discussion, the most sensitive factors at issue deal with the possibility that the current structure and language of accountability may lead to counterproductive behavior. For the citizen, it is critical that accountability not be used as a weapon in moving the school establishment in directions which are dictated not by concern for the child, but by political and social pressure. For the educator, it is critical that concern for some of the more abrasive aspects dealt with under the general heading of accountability do not become a justification for self-protective behavior or for "locking out" the parent and concerned nonprofessional. Ultimately, the forces that have fostered accountability and the genuine commitment of most school professionals should enable both groups to avoid confrontation and to direct a cooperative effort toward maximizing children's learning opportunities.

## Notes

1. Public Law 94-142, The Education for All Handicapped Children Act (Reston, Va.: Council for Exceptional Children, 1976).

2. See Scottie Torres, ed., *A Primer on Individualized Education Programs* for Handicapped Children (Reston, Va.: The Foundation for Exceptional Children, 1977). [ED 136 453]

3. Specifically, according to Public Law 93-380, Title VII, Section 705 (1974) and the Educational Amendments Act of 1974.

4. See Leon Lesinger, *Every Kid a Winner: Accountability in Education* (New York: Simon & Schuster, Inc., 1970).

5. Kenneth Goodman, "Testing in Reading: A General Critique," in Robert B. Ruddell, ed., *Accountability and Reading Instruction: Critical Issues* (Urbana, Ill.: National Council of Teachers of English, 1973), pp. 21-34; and Richard E. Hodges, "Some Assumptions about Behavioral Objectives as Related to Reading," ibid., pp. 13-20. [ED 073 448]

6. James Laffey, "Accountability: A Brief History and Analysis," in *Accountability and Reading Instruction*, pp. 1-13.

7. See H. Rutherford Turnbull III, "Accountability: An Overview of the Impact of Litigation on Professionals," *Exceptional Children* 41 (1975): 427-33.

8. Gene E. Brophy and Thomas Good, "How Teachers View Accountability," *Phi Delta Kappan* 55 (1975): 73-75.

9. Harold L. Herber, "Accountability: A Summary Statement," in *Accountability and Reading Instruction*, pp. 45-47.

10. John Brademas, in an address at Memphis State University, reported in *The Congressional Record*, 10 December 1973.

# READING ABILITY AS A GRADUATION REQUIREMENT: Some Legal Aspects

ROBERT E. DRABA*

Confronted with the problem of seniors graduating from high school without rudimentary skills in reading, some school systems have proposed that reading ability be used as a graduation requirement.[1] But if this requirement is fairly and consistently applied, some graduating seniors will be denied diplomas. Given the "see you in court" complex that afflicts many, school systems might reasonably expect these students to make use of either the due process or equal protection clauses of the Fourteenth Amendment to challenge the procedures used to deny diplomas or the methods used to classify students according to reading ability.

*Procedural Due Process*

The Fourteenth Amendment provides that no state shall "deprive any person of life, liberty and property without due process of the law." If a school system denies diplomas without providing minimal procedural safeguards, the affected students may challenge this in court, arguing that since the denial of a diploma impinges upon interests of liberty and property, due process is required. Such an argument might be successful, given the language of the United States Supreme Court opinion in *Goss* v. *Lopez*, a case which established the due-process rights of students threatened with short suspension.[2]

In this case, the Court observed that students have property interests in their educations and liberty interests in their reputations; thus, to deprive a student of educational benefits and reputation without due process of the

---

*Robert E. Draba is a member of the associate faculty at Indiana University Northwest.

law violates the Constitution. According to this precedent, a student can legally contest the denial of a diploma.

Some might argue that the requirement of due process for short suspensions cannot be extended to the denial of a diploma, because the suspension represents a sanction for violating a regulation, whereas the denial of a diploma is, strictly speaking, neither sanction nor punishment. But the Supreme Court has previously required procedural safeguards where a noncriminal stigma was involved.[3] Moreover, four justices dissented in *Goss* partly because they felt that the majority holding might be extended to other "claims of impairment of one's education entitlement." Finally, two courts have required that the placement of a child in special education classes be preceded by a formal hearing if the parents disagree with the placement.[4] Certainly, the placement of students into a group denied diplomas is as serious and also requires safeguards.[5] But what safeguards?

To predict the safeguards that courts might require in the case of denying a student a diploma is difficult. Precise procedural safeguards depend upon the circumstances and the interests involved.[6] In general, however, "the standard is whether [the student] has been treated with fundamental fairness in light of total circumstances."[7] Given the circumstances and interests involved in such a denial, "fundamental fairness" requires not one, but two, sets of safeguards.

The first set of safeguards is derived from the purpose of the policy. Although a policy which denies a diploma to students who fail to demonstrate reading proficiency has many functions, the overriding purpose is to promote the acquisition of reading skills by making the consequences of not acquiring such skills very dramatic. At first, it seems as if this policy places all the burden upon the student; however, given the purpose of the policy—to promote the acquisition of reading skills—it is clear that a distinct burden also rests upon teachers and administrators. Educators must organize to identify, early and systematically, those students who need help in reading and must provide the opportunity for students to develop the skills required for graduation. The objective of teachers and administrators can only be to insure that every student who is physically and mentally able to meet the requirements does so. Therefore, to be fair to students, school systems might well consider implementing the following safeguards:

1. Identifying students who are unable to meet reading requirements by no later than their second year of high school.
2. Notifying these students and their parents of this fact.
3. Holding conferences and explaining to parents the student's current status and the options available for remediation.
4. Providing opportunities for remediation.
5. Making regular progress reports to students and parents.

Although these long-term safeguards are novel as requirements of due process, they would insure that each student would be treated with "fundamental fairness in light of total circumstances."

Actually, although these procedures seem innovative, they do have precedent. Even though the United States Supreme Court has held that utility companies and states are not "sufficiently connected" to satisfy the "state action" requirement of a due process claim under the Fourteenth Amendment, invariably, utilities provide service termination notices to those behind in their payments.[8] One purpose of these notices is to encourage payment.[9] Clearly, the utility would rather receive its money than terminate service, and hence, gives the customer a chance to pay.

Just as the utility company gives the customer an opportunity to retain service by providing early warning and ample time to pay, the school should give the student an opportunity to earn a diploma by providing early warning and ample time to learn to read. Therefore, if the purpose of the reading requirement is to encourage students to acquire reading skills, schools should warn students of possible problems several years before graduation.[10]

It is inevitable that some students will not meet these requirements, even though opportunities for remediation are provided over an extended period of time. In these cases, a more familiar set of safeguards should be provided to insure fundamental fairness.[11] At the very least, the student should be given written notice of the system's intent to deny the diploma and should be asked to attend a hearing with his or her parents, preceded by counsel to review the evidence supporting the denial. An opportunity during the hearing should be provided to present evidence of reading proficiency, if the school system's classification method is in question. If the hearing officer believes that the student deserves further testing to satisfy any remaining doubts about ability, he or she should involve reading specialists or psychometricians; the final decision should be evaluated in light of all new information. Finally, the student should retain the right to appeal the decision and should be given the opportunity to return at some later date, demonstrate reading proficiency, and receive his or her diploma. Even though these safeguards seem elaborate and time-consuming, they protect the student from the unwarranted denial of a diploma. Clearly, this should be the primary concern of the school system.

It is difficult to imagine a school system that would make graduation conditional upon reading ability without providing careful measures to ensure accuracy and fairness. Hopefully, those systems planning to use reading proficiency as a graduation requirement have carefully considered and plan to implement the kinds of safeguards recommended here. If not, they should expect to see themselves in court.

*Equal Protection*

The equal protection clause of the Fourteenth Amendment provides that "no state shall . . . deny to any person within its jurisdiction the equal protection of the laws." But the demand for equal protection does not mean that the laws must be applied equally to all citizens within a state. State legislatures and their creations, like school boards, may classify persons for differential treatment; however, they may not treat people differently "who are similarly situated with respect to the purpose of the law."[12]

Although the equal protection clause may permit a school system to classify and treat students differently on the basis of their reading abilities, the clause demands that all students with the same reading ability be treated the same. To satisfy this demand, the system must employ a classification method which precisely separates students only on the basis of their reading abilities. So often, though, a grouping scheme based upon a classification method like a test has an adverse and disproportionate impact upon minority students: they frequently seem to be unfairly represented in the lower ranks of a tracking scheme[13] or in classes for the educable mentally retarded.[14] And, even though the court is reluctant to interfere with the policies and practices of school boards[15] and generally supports the right of a board to group children for differential treatment,[16] several courts have prohibited particular grouping schemes based upon specific tests because, in their opinion, these tests were biased against minority students.[17]

If a school system with substantial numbers of minority students uses reading ability as a graduation requirement, it would not be surprising to find that lower-class minority students are disproportionately represented in the group of students denied a diploma.

In 1969, Rosalind Landes prepared a concise report for the First National City Bank of New York entitled "Public Education in New York City."[18] The report revealed that in three regular academic high schools, where two-thirds or more of the graduates received general diplomas (often sarcastically called "certificates of attendance"), the student body was predominantly black and Puerto Rican. Three high schools with the lowest percentage of general diplomas awarded were predominantly Caucasian. Landes also indicated that, overall, black and Puerto Rican students received a disproportionately high percentage of general diplomas, awarded on the basis of their performance on the New York State Regents Examination. (Conversely, a disproportionate percentage of Caucasian students received academic diplomas.) Some students may choose as the basis of their challenge the fact that the classification method discriminates on the basis of race and therefore violates the equal protection clause of the Fourteenth Amendment.

The original concern of the equal protection clause was to prevent racial discrimination.[19] The court has remained faithful to this purpose by generally prohibiting enactments or policies which use race as an explicit classifying factor[20] and those which use otherwise neutral classifying facts that discriminate on the basis of race.[21] But the United States Supreme Court refuses to prohibit a law or an official act solely because it has a "racially disproportionate" impact.[22] This does not mean, however, that unless lower-class, minority students can show that the school system has intentionally used a reading test to discriminate invidiously against them, they cannot challenge the classification method in court under the equal protection clause. Courts often apply a more "searching judicial inquiry" to enactments or policies which prejudice against "discrete and insular minorities.[23] Even the Supreme Court agrees that the differential effect of a test on racial groups may call for "further inquiry" by the court.[24] What form might this further inquiry take?

Before *Washington* v. *Davis*, a recent testing case that discourages the practice of shifting the burden of justification to the defendants in equal protection litigation, the form that further inquiry would take was quite clear. Courts confronted with tests having adverse and disproportionate impacts upon minorities have gained their doctrinal bearings from *Hobson* v. *Hansen* and *Griggs* v. *Duke Power Company*.[25]

An element of the *Hobson* decision that has influenced the approach taken in testing cases is the *prima facie* showing of a racially disproportionate impact, which leads to shifting the burden of justification to the defendants. In this case, Judge J. Skelly Wright has stated that "a precipitating cause of the constitutional inquiry in this case is the fact that those being consigned to the lower tracks are the poor and the Negroes, whereas the upper tracks are the provinces of the more affluent and the whites." These "unmistakable signs of invidious discrimination" imposed upon the defendants, according to Judge Wright, "a weighty burden of explaining why the poor and the Negro should be those who populate the lower ranks of the track system." Moreover, he stated that "the element of deliberate discrimination is . . . not one of the requisites of an equal protection violation." Previous to *Hobson*, courts generally required that a disproportionate racial impact be traced to some discriminatory intent.[26] Even though Judge Wright proclaimed that deliberate discrimination was not a prerequisite to a violation, he did not overturn the track system solely because the classification method—standardized aptitude tests—had a disproportionate racial impact; he overturned it because the defendants could not effectively show that the tests were rationally related to the purpose of the track system. He found the tests to be culturally biased; thus, they classified students by their socioeconomic and racial status instead of their "ability to learn."

The Supreme Court reinforced Judge Wright's basic approach in *Griggs* v.

*Duke Power Company*. There, the Court held that Title VII of the 1964 Civil Rights Act

> requires the elimination of artificial, arbitrary, and unnecessary barriers to employment that operate invidiously to discriminate on the basis of race, and, if as here, an employment practice that operates to exclude Negroes cannot be shown to be related to job performance, it is prohibited, notwithstanding the employer's lack of discriminatory intent.

Even though this case was not decided under the equal protection clause, it was often cited in equal protection cases to support shifting the burden of proof to the defendants and requiring them to show that the test used was related to the purpose of the grouping scheme.[27]

*Hobson* and *Griggs* established the form that further inquiry might take in a situation in which minority students claimed that the classification method violated the equal protection clause. Even though no intentional discrimination was involved, the court might be expected to shift the burden to the defendants upon proof of disproportionate racial impact. The board would then have to show, for example, that the reading test used to classify students was rationally related to the purpose of the reading requirement.[28] But then, *Washington* v. *Davis*, an equal protection case involving the use of a test with disproportionate racial impact, was decided.

In *Washington*, the Supreme Court declared: "We have never held that the constitutional standard for adjudicating claims of invidious racial discrimination is identical to standards applicable under Title VII and we decline to do so today." Later, the Court stated the following: "We are not disposed to adopt this more rigorous standard [the *Griggs* approach] for the purposes of applying the Fifth and the Fourteenth Amendments in cases such as this." Finally, the Court voiced its disagreement with lower court cases which "rested on or expressed the view that proof of discriminatory racial purpose is unnecessary in making out an equal protection violation." Such language seems to doom any testing case which cannot trace disproportionate impact to a discriminatory intent. Since those school systems which plan to make graduation conditional upon reading ability clearly do not intend to use a test in order to discriminate, it might be concluded from *Washington* that minority students cannot successfully challenge the classification method used by the system. This, however, is not an accurate conclusion.

*Washington* established that a more probing standard of review is not required in an equal protection case solely because the classification method has a disproportionate racial impact; intentional discrimination triggers a more probing standard. In the context of a testing case, this means that a court cannot shift the burden of justification to the defendants simply because the test has an adverse impact upon minorities. *Washington* reasserted, then, the so-called "restrained standard of review," which defers to the reasonable actions of state officials and requires the plaintiffs to show that a classification method, like a reading test, is not rationally related to the purpose of law.[29]

To show that the school system's classification method is not rationally related to the purpose of making graduation conditional upon reading ability requires the plaintiffs to show that the method used is biased against minorities. Obviously, the ability to show bias depends upon the test used, the technique employed to detect bias, and the extent of the impact on racial groups. But, given the aversion of many to the use of tests to classify students,[30] the many and varied techniques for detecting bias,[31] and the shortcomings of traditional techniques for test construction,[32] it would not be an overwhelming task to generate "evidence" to show that a given classification method discriminates on the basis of race and therefore does not rationally relate to the purpose of the reading requirement. Whether this "evidence" and argument would convince a court depends in large measure on the response of the defendant—the school system.

Traditionally, the court would accept from the state any set of facts which would justify the use of the classification.[33] The Burger Court, however, has strayed from such deference and has demonstrated a tendency to examine whether a classifying fact has a fair and substantial relationship to the purpose of the law. This approach, sometimes called "the restrained standard with bite," means, for example, that a student's reading score—the classifying fact—must be related to his or her reading ability; in short, the classification method must be "valid."[34]

If plaintiffs presented evidence of test bias, the school system, if it expected to maintain the use of the classification method, would have to present evidence of test validity. This burden, however, would not follow exclusively from a disproportionate racial impact (as it would under *Griggs*), but from the court's desire to ascertain whether the classification method has a fair and substantial relationship to the purpose of the graduation requirement. This would not only conform to the new, restrained standard but also to the dicta of *Washington*. And if, for example, the school system did not show test validity and the plaintiffs did show test bias, a court would probably prohibit the use of the test and have few doctrinal difficulties in doing so.

Of course, that all evidence would be on only one side of the question is doubtful.[35] Most likely, systems planning to use reading ability in this manner would have already established the validity of their classification methods, and this could be used to counter the claims of the plaintiffs. Whether this evidence would overcome a sound and spirited attack on the specific classification method is, however, uncertain.[36]

In general, the court tends to uphold classification methods having some "reasonable basis,"[37] but it often demands more than a "reasonable basis" when the method affects the educational interests of minority students.[38]

In *Washington*, the Supreme Court listed over fifteen cases in various contexts where the lower courts demanded "some justification going substantially beyond what would be necessary to validate most other legislative classifications." The Court then stated the following: "With all due respect, to the extent that these cases rested on or expressed the view that proof of discriminatory racial purpose is unnecessary in making out an equal protection violation, we are in disagreement." Yet the justices omitted all educational testing cases including *Hobson*, which was cited in several cases listed by the Court. Whether these omissions signal the Court's approval of the approach taken in *Hobson* is unclear; one might speculate, though, that they do.

As noted earlier, in *Hobson*, Judge Wright proscribed the use of aptitude tests because they were not rationally related to the purpose of the tracking scheme. The more demanding restrained standard applied by him might also be characterized as the "restrained standard with bite" employed by the Court in recent equal protection cases.[39] Therefore, even though the defendant school system presented evidence of test "validity," a court might nevertheless proscribe its use because the evidence was not sufficient to show a rational relationship or because the evidence presented by the plaintiffs was sufficient to show bias. This possibility leads to a vexing problem for courts: what psychometric and statistical criteria should be used to resolve a conflict caused by competing claims about classification methods?

A review of the literature reveals that there is no quick and clear technique to detect test bias. Unfortunately, differences between methods lead to correspondingly different results, making the detection of bias a confusing undertaking.[40] In a case challenging reading classification methods, the lack of a standard to ascertain whether bias in the classification method exists might force the court to make a heuristic decision about the competing evidence.[41] Clearly, what is needed is a definitive procedure for detecting bias.[42] But until one is available, courts will continue to hear testing cases and decide them as best they can.

Finally, a school system that believes it can deny students diplomas on the basis of reading ability and not have its classification method challenged in court is, at best, naive. Long before the first senior is denied a diploma, the system should gather as much evidence as possible regarding the validity and objectivity of its classification method and stand ready to defend it, not only to the courts, but also to members of the system itself.

### Notes

1. See "Gary High Schools Eye Graduation Tests," *Chicago Tribune*, 17 October 1974 and "Los Angeles Tightens Up—Graduates Must Read," *Chicago Sun-Times*, 7 January 1976.

2. 419 U.S. 565 (1975).

3. In *Wisconsin* v. *Constantineau*, 400 U.S. 433 (1970).

4. *Pennsylvania Association for Retarded Children* v. *Commonwealth of Pennsylvania*, 343 F. Supp. 279 (1972); and *Mills* v. *Board of Education*, 348 F. Supp. 866 (1972).

5. For a discussion of this, see David Kirp et al., "Legal Reform of Special Education: Empirical Studies and Procedural Proposals," *California Law Review* 62 (1974): 40.

6. *Dixon* v. *Alabama State Board of Education*, 294 F. 2d 150 (1961).

7. M. Chester Nolte, "Due Process: Where It's Taking Boards and How Yours Can Get There Safely," *American School Board Journal* 159 (1971): 36.

8. *Jackson* v. *Metropolitan Edison Company*, 419 U.S. 345 (1974).

9. *Palmer* v. *Columbia Gas Company of Ohio*, 342 F. Supp. 241 (1972).

10. The parents of Peter Doe alleged that the school system "should have given [them] some notice of his reading deficiency . . ." ["Judge Dismisses Peter Doe Case: Martinez Confident of Reversal," *Phi Delta Kappan* 56 (1974): 227.]

11. Notice and a hearing are considered to be traditional requirements of due process. For a concise discussion, see *Fuentes* v. *Shevin*, 407 U.S. 67 at 80-82 (1971).

12. See Joseph Tussman and Jacobus tenBroek, "Equal Protection of the Laws," *California Law Review* 37 (1949): 346.

13. *Hobson* v. *Hansen*, 269 F. Supp. 401 (1967).

14. *Larry P.* v. *Riles*, 343 F. Supp. 1306 (1972).

15. See *Tinker* v. *Des Moines School District*, 393 U.S. 503 at 507 (1969); and *Eppersons* v. *Arkansas*, 393 U.S. 97 at 104 (1968).

16. *Hobson*; and *Larry P.*

17. For a review of some of these cases, see Paul Weckstein, "Legal Challenges to Educational Testing Practices," *Inequality in Education* 15 (1973): 92 and Paul Tractenberg and Elaine Jacoby, "Pupil Testing: A Legal View, Report No. 38." (Princeton: ERIC Clearinghouse on Tests, Measurement, and Evaluation, 1974). [ED 102 211]

18. Rosalind Landes, "Public Education in New York City" (New York: First National City Bank, 1969). [ED 044 458]

19. Ferdinand P. Schoettle, "The Equal Protection Clause in Public Education," *Columbia Law Review* 71 (1971): 1364.

20. *Bolling* v. *Sharpe*, 347 U.S. 497 (1954).

21. *Hunter* v. *Erickson*, 393 U.S. 385 (1969); and *Yick Ho* v. *Hopkins*, 118 U.S. 356 (1886).

22. *Washington* v. *Davis*, 44 *United States Law Week* 4789, 8 June 1976.

23. *United States* v. *Caroline Products*, 304 U.S.144 (1938).

24. *Washington* v. *Davis*.

25. *Griggs* v. *Duke Power Company*, 401 U.S. 424 (1970).

26. See Harold W. Horowitz, "Unseparate But Unequal—The Emerging Fourteenth amendment Issue in Public School Education," *UCLA Law Review* 13 (1966): 1151.

27. See *Larry P.* v. *Riles*.

28. See James V. Dick, "Equal Protection and Intelligence Classifications," *Stanford Law Review* 26 (1974): 663-70.

29. Under this standard, the classification method "bears a presumption of validity" [Comments: "Educational Financing, Equal Protection of the Laws and the Supreme Court," *Michigan Law Review* 70 (1972): 1331].

30. See *Testing* (Washington, D.C.: National Education Association, 1973) [ED 087 254]; and Robert I. Williams, "Black Pride, Academic Relevance, and Individual Achievement,"

in R. Tyler and R. Wolf, eds., *Crucial Issues in Testing*, (Berkeley, Cal.: McCutchan Publishing Corporation, 1974), pp. 13-20.

31. R. F. Potthoff, "Statistical Aspects of the Problem of Biases in Psychological Tests," (Chapel Hill, N.C.: University of North Carolina, Institute of Statistics, Mimeo Series No. 479, 1966).

32. See John R. Bormuth, "Reading Literacy: Its Definition and Assessment," *Reading Research Quarterly* 9 (1973-74): 35-41; and Benjamin D. Wright, "Sample-free Test Calibration and Person Measurement," in *Proceedings of the 1967 Invitational Conference on Testing Problems* (Princeton, N.J.: Educational Testing Service, 1968).

33. *Lindsley* v. *Natural Carbonic Gas Co.*, 220 U.S. 61 (1911).

34. Gerald Gunther, "The Supreme Court 1971 Term, Foreward—In Search of Evolving Doctrine on a Changing Court: A Model for a Newer Equal Protection," *Harvard Law Review* 86 (1972): 1-48.

35. Although *Larry P.* v. *Riles* would seem to indicate otherwise.

36. See *Hobson* v. *Hansen*.

37. *F. S. Royster Guano Co.* v. *Virginia*, 253 U.S. 412 at 415 (1920).

38. In *Keyes* v. *School District No. 1*, 93 S. Ct. 2686 (1973), the Court indicated that "it is both fair and reasonable to require that the school authorities bear the burden of showing that their actions . . . were not motivated by segregative intent." (As quoted by Michael S. Sorgen, "Testing and Tracking in Public Schools," *The Hastings Law Journal*, 24 (1973): 1153.

39. See *Reed* v. *Reed*, 404 U.S. 71 (1971).

40. Janice Scheuneman, "A New Method of Assessing Bias in Test Items," a paper presented at the 1975 convention of the American Educational Research Association, Washington, D.C. [ED 106 359]

41. In employment cases, the court can defer to the "Equal Employment Opportunity Commission Guidelines on Employee Selection Procedures." See, for example, *Federal Register*, Vol. 35, No. 149—1 August 1970, p. 12333.

42. Although no "definitive" procedure currently exists, the analysis of residuals from the Rasch logistic response model may provide a coherent set of definitive procedures. Benjamin D. Wright of The University of Chicago and his student, Ronald J. Mead, are investigating this approach to the detection and correction of test bias. Preliminary results seem encouraging. (See Benjamin D. Wright and Ronald J. Mead, "Analysis of Residuals from the Rasch Model"; and Ronald J. Mead, "Assessing the Fit of Data to the Rasch Model," papers presented at the 1976 convention of the American Educational Research Association, San Francisco.)

# WHAT KIND OF READING
# WILL THE LAW PRESCRIBE?

WILLIAM D. PAGE*

In the long-term quest to generate a literate society in the United States, law and education persistently interact. This is as it should be, for the precise discourses of law and education share an important touchstone: both are prescriptive. Specifically, they tell what should be, rather than exclusively what was, what is, or what will be, if certain conditions prevail. Educational discourse is concerned with what should happen to people, particularly to youngsters as they grow to adulthood. Laws tell us what our legislators, courts, and rulemakers have agreed upon, and, with our consent as voters, how we should act.

Today, more than ever before, proposals are afoot to prescribe, by law, how youngsters should perform in reading at various designated grade levels. In part because of the attention drawn by court cases, sharp focus is on promotion procedures and on graduation requirements.

When the laws that society agrees upon are broken, a penalty is extracted from the lawbreaker. But who will pay the penalty when a child does not meet the reading requirement for graduation from high school? First, the denied student will pay a penalty by not receiving his or her diploma. Second, the student may extract a penalty from his or her school system—board of education members, school administrators, or teachers. Third, taxpayers will pay a penalty, because tax monies will finance the long, troublesome period required for exploration of problems in court, a process where educators will become familiar with legal problems and lawyers will become aware of educational problems. These penalties must be compared with the benefits that

*William D. Page is an associate professor affiliated with the Department of Secondary Education's Reading Study Center at the University of Connecticut, Storrs.

might accrue to students as a result of changes in instruction. It is not certain whether education is legally a right, a privilege, or both.[1] When issues in reading are considered, some difficult problems of definition are brought to the surface. Until we, as a society, through our lawmaking provisions, can agree on whether education is a right, a privilege, or both, we face the same quandry with regard to the definition of reading.

## Hidden Issues in Reading

If reading performance is to be used as a legal tool, then an accurate way to gauge reading performance must be used. Those not familiar with the issues in reading often assume that determining levels of reading performance is simply a case of administering a reading test. However, reading tests differ according to the definitions of reading itself that they assume. Furthermore, there is ample evidence that our most widely accepted reading tests do not test what we want them to test.[2] And, what reading measures do test is subject to sufficient error to suggest they may prove unmanageable in the legal arena. Although the issues in reading are familiar to reading experts, they seem to be hidden from many others in both law and education. Several issues are discussed here to demonstrate the scope of the problems involved in deciding the legal fate of individuals on the basis of their scores on reading tests.

Generally, three classes of reading theories are identifiable in the literature: one group of views centers on the production of a spoken analogue to print; a second group of views involves reconstructing the author's message, either syntactically, semantically, or both; and the third class of views suggests that the construction of knowledge about the author's message is essential.

## Toward a Spoken Analogue

Underlying the idea that reading is the production of a spoken analogue to the print is the notion that reading may be conceived of in a number of related ways. One such view of reading asserts that sounds represent the surface characteristics of print by recoding orthography into phonology. Components of this hypothesis are represented in "reading" tests that focus on associating meaningless sounds with meaningless letters and letter combinations. Another component involves testing the ability to say a word when the word is presented in isolation from other language.

It is unlikely that society will permit long-term tenure of laws based on the "spoken-analogue" definition of reading, because the performance that such tests measure falls far short of what is commonly understood as reading. We can speculate, however, that the first primitive attempts to apply law to reading performance will probably reflect one or another of these components, because simpler forms of performance can be more efficiently and reliably tested than more complex forms.

Enough people in our society read and know from their own experiences how printed messages are used to suggest that this view of reading will not stand up under critical analysis in court situations. Imagine, for example, the reactions of the lawyer and the parents of a youngster who can make sense of most printed messages, but who is denied promotion or graduation on the basis of a phonics test. Conversely, simply because a youngster can produce a spoken analogue of printed language, with no demonstration of comprehension, does not mean that he or she can read.

Defendants of this theory might suggest that a reader must be able to perform these skills in order to read and, in fact, in order to learn to read. However, few people who do read, in the general sense of the word, are able to demonstrate knowledge of very many of over 160 basic phonics generalizations.[3] Although some theorists assert that proficient readers knew these principles at one time, but have forgotten them, this has not been shown empirically. Too many youngsters who already read come to school with little or no formal phonics instruction to permit us to believe that these skills are prerequisites for reading.

Other critics maintain that an examination of every letter is a prerequisite for obtaining meaning from print, but the sum of evidence supporting this conclusion is not persuasive. At first encounter, the spoken-analogue view appeals to common sense. However, the courts will find controversy, and society will probably object, simply because too many individuals perceive a more complex relationship between printed language and its spoken derivative.

## Reconstructing the Author's Message

Another theory of reading involves relationships between the language of the author and the language of the reader. Here, the reader is viewed as being engaged in a process of reconstructing the author's meaning or message. The reconstruction may be viewed as syntactic, semantic, or both. Tests based on a syntactic view may ask a reader to demonstrate comprehension by requiring a syntactic reconstruction. (For example, if a given sentence reads "Barramb barroped the barrip," and the question to be answered is "What was barroped?," one can answer "The barrip," without really understanding the content of the message.)

A second, similar view is semantically based. Semantic reconstructionists sometimes view reading as obtaining meaning from individual words and blending the words together to form the sense of a sentence. Little empirical evidence supports this idea.

A third view also involves reconstruction of the author's message: the printed word is comprehended through the total contextual fabric of the author's language, along with the linguistic knowledge of the reader in a combined syntactic, semantic, and experiential effort. This last view most closely approximates the lay person's understanding of reading.

Basically, then, society expects youngsters to learn to reconstruct the meaning of messages from printed language. Lawmakers and courts should find this conception of reading—the semantic and syntactic reconstruction of the author's message—useful in mustering support. Unfortunately, however, it too is problematic. Presently, most widely used tests of reading comprehension fall short of measuring whether the meaning of the author's message is actually reconstructed. The quest for efficiency has driven test makers to paper-and-pencil solutions which confound both the task of writing and the task of remembering with indicators of comprehension.[4]

The validity of other reading comprehension tests is also in question. Many questions in "reading comprehension" tests can be answered without even reading the text to which the questions refer.[5] This may be accomplished through the interpretation of syntactic patterns evident in the questions. In addition, even time-consuming informal reading inventory procedures fall short of achieving the validity required to make legal decisions.[6] An augmented informal reading inventory can come closer to reaching this goal if administered by a well-trained interpreter of reading performance, but each step toward increased construct validity also increases the time investment and reduces efficiency.

Current educational litigation will affect millions of youngsters, making inefficient assessment procedures infeasible. There are not enough reading specialists to cope with such a task, and the facilities for preparing such individuals—universities—are presently engaged in the scramble to reduce training capacities and expenditures in order to cope with declining enrollments.

### Constructive Views

Although to some, the semantic and syntactic reconstruction of the meaning of a message may seem adequate as a definition of reading, as an educational goal, it too falls short of what society expects of high school graduates. Yet another view of reading holds that the reader constructs his or her own personal knowledge of the author's message after reconstructing the meaning. This view takes into consideration factors of application and evaluation. Here, the reader might be expected to be able to remember and apply constructed knowledge in the identification, creation, and solution of problems. Furthermore, the reader would be expected to distinguish truth from falsity, fact from opinion, and so on. The appreciation of literature is a key component of many high school English curricula in this regard, invoking the application of values not only to the denotative concepts of writing, but to the qualitative characteristics of language and to the discernment of the author's purposes and uses of literary technique.[7]

This view of reading is characterized by many, including some reading experts, as a case of thinking, not reading. It is not argued here that constructing knowledge in relation to reading is, or is not, reading. The formation of such critical awareness is, however, an important educational goal and one that society expects to be accomplished. Youngsters must not be caught in the trap of being able to understand what an author means without having the tools to permit them to evaluate the content of the message. We must teach our youngsters that the fact that something is in print is not reason enough to believe it. If legal provisions reflect the bias expressed here, views of reading underlying the law will have to reflect the definition of reading as the reconstruction of meaning, embrace the educational goal that our students learn to construct personal knowledge of messages they read, and encourage the evaluation of message content.

A major difficulty with applying this view is that the present machinery of testing is moving in the opposite direction. It is time consuming to assess readers' reactions to printed messages when the concern is both for getting *and* evaluating the message. To reduce time investments in assessment, evaluators tend to focus on those aspects of reading that are easily and efficiently testable. Hence, the desire for efficiency drives us toward the spoken-analogue views and away from ideas involving meaning, knowledge, and comprehension. The road back from the spoken-analogue views becomes longer with each attempt to establish accountability in reading instruction without critical examination of the underlying definitions of reading. The quest for efficiency in testing is counterproductive to the attempt to create legally useful assessments of reading; we need every scrap of information we can get to make an assessment that approaches the degree of validity necessary in a court of law.

Although perhaps the controversies in reading cannot be exhausted, the views expressed here reflect major metaphors underlying conceptions of reading itself. Any serious legal proposal regarding student performance must reflect assumptions about the kind of reading that is desirable. No simple mandate of grade level, without attention to these presuppositions, can do anything but create problems. The evidence to support this prediction will be upon us soon, if it is not already.

## Productive Possibilities

The situation, however, is far from hopeless. Laws can still do much to help improve reading, as they have in the United States by simply requiring public education. There are several clearly productive paths, no matter what the outcomes of mandated achievement levels may be. The underlying purpose of these proposals is the same—to provide better instruction. Instead of threatening court suits to get teachers and school administrators to improve performance, these methods seek to help educators by upgrading their skills and knowledge.

One such proposal is simply to increase the amount of preparation in reading instruction required by law for certification. The present state of teacher education in this country produces elementary teachers who, for the most part, have taken only one course in the methods and materials of language arts and reading instruction. (Sometimes this is bolstered by a course in children's literature.) At the secondary level, English teachers in some states are required to take only one course in teaching reading. Most states do not even require this, and most other subject areas also require no work at all in reading instruction. This regrettable circumstance is supported by the licensing procedures of most states; the result is that most elementary and secondary teachers who are responsible for helping youngsters learn to read know very little about reading instruction. Legislators can obviously change this by increasing the number of reading instruction courses required for certification. (In many states, the implementation of one required course can increase the amount of preparation for reading instruction by 100 percent.)

A second area where the law can productively intervene is in personnel hiring practices. Although in most states, certification laws appear to indicate that teachers must meet minimum certification requirements, loopholes exist. Provisions for special problems, special instances, and special groups may invoke similarly special hiring practices. A special program represents a politically volatile situation: in the eyes of the program founders it may seem essential that the program appear to be underway, even if appropriately trained personnel are not available. A special program may also be established with a promise to hire the best qualified personnel available. This may actually result in the hiring of people who are the best available, but it may also result in hiring personnel who do not meet minimum standards of certification. It is of some importance that the salaries of uncertified personnel are usually lower than certified personnel. Legislation can readily remove such loopholes—and the time is ripe, because presently, there is a surplus of teachers who qualify for certification. Tightening loopholes in hiring practices will, however, cost money simply because qualified people must be paid according to negotiated salary levels.

A third proposal to improve services encourages upgrading the skills of practicing teachers. Laws can prescribe that practicing teachers seek further training in reading instruction. Presently, the demand for teachers is declining as a result of parallel declines in the number of school-age "war babies." As this trend persists, it provides additional motivation for teachers to improve their skills in order to keep their jobs. Universities are equipped for large numbers of past students and can be called upon to provide such inservice training. Before the educational machinery of the last few decades is disassembled, we should consider the possibility of using the existing facilities and personnel to improve the teaching of reading.

A fourth proposal for improvement is similarly related to the changes in school population sizes due to declining enrollments. Class size may be reduced, particularly at the lower grade-levels where reading instruction presently begins. No controversial search for empirical support is required to determine the difference between a class of thirty-five and a class of fifteen students. Statistical evidence to support the effectiveness of class size reduction is, however, scanty, perhaps in part because of the error factors in the standardized tests most often used as the basis of judgment. However, an obvious outcome of reduced class size is increased individual attention, a factor long known by remedial reading specialists to be instrumental in helping youngsters learn to read.[8] Legislation can prescribe class size. Of course, reducing class size requires additional expenditures, but neither will mandating reading levels be inexpensive.

The proposals suggested here lack the dramatic appeal of mandating levels of performance. Drab as they may be, the proposals outlined above are reasonable and promise a greater long-term impact on reading instruction than can be expected from mandated levels of performance.

## Reconsiderations

Only a superficial analysis of the problems surrounding teacher certification, school populations, and teacher education is provided in this discussion. These areas are exceedingly complex, but compared to the difficulties that mandating levels of reading performance will engender, they provide a more reliably productive direction. Viewed economically, any change in mandated levels or in other areas will cost money.

The next decade will see important changes in the relationship between law and education. Reading is destined to be in the limelight as a target for simplistic legal proposals, at least until parents, lawyers, and economists begin to grasp the complexity of the reading process. Legal proposals will abound. Court cases will tell the tale for a while, and many will pay penalties.

Will the mandated reading-level approach help youngsters to read better? We cannot tell yet. How will the type and degree of performance be specified? First attempts will probably center on presently available standardized tests. What root metaphors will the public grasp onto and drive the legislators to use? We probably will see an early focus on easily tested tasks that reflect the spoken-analogue view. Can we hold one group of people responsible for the way another group thinks? For a while, we can pretend to do this, but no one has yet devised a way to accomplish this in a democratic society. If reading is believed to involve thinking in some sense, legislating thinking is what is being proposed with mandated reading levels. What are the hidden economic and psychological penalties in store for youngsters who fail to perform at mandated levels? These are also unknown. What provisions can be made for those who fail? Here, we have a rich body of information to draw upon in the literature of remedial reading instruction, but we must accept the fact that the task is complex and will be expensive. The answers to these questions may tell the future of hundreds of superintendents, school board members, school administrators, and lawyers; thousands of teachers; and millions of children.

## Notes

1. Although law in the state of Michigan, by virtue of its free-textbook policy, suggests that it is a right (Michigan State Constitution, Article 8, Section 2).

2. Ralph Tyler and Richard Wolf, *Crucial Issues in Testing* (Berkely, Cal.: McCutchan Publishing Co., 1974).

3. For a discussion of these generalizations, see Frank Smith, *Understanding Reading: A Psycholinguistic Analysis of Learning and Learning to Read* (New York: Holt, Rinehart and Winston, 1971), p. 170.

4. John Carroll, "Defining Language Comprehension: Some Speculations," in R. Freedle and J. Carroll, eds., *Language Comprehension and the Acquisition of Knowledge* (Washington, D.C.: V. H. Winston and Sons, 1972), pp. 1-29.

5. J. Jaap Tuinman. "Determining the Passage Dependency of Comprehension Questions in Five Major Texts," *Reading Research Quarterly* 9 (1973): 206-23.

6. W. Powell and C. Dunkeld, "Validity of IRI Reading Levels," *Elementary English* 48 (1971): 637-42.

7. See Thomas Barrett's "Taxonomy of Reading Comprehension," in Thomas Barrett, *Reading 360 Monograph* (Lexington, Mass.: Ginn and Company, 1972); and Richard Smith and Thomas Barrett, *Teaching Reading in the Middle Grades* (Reading, Mass: Addison-Wesley Publishing Co., 1974).

8. Guy Bond and Miles Tinker, *Reading Difficulties: Their Diagnosis and Correction* (Englewood Cliffs, N.J.: Prentice-Hall, Inc., 1973).

# THE LEGAL OBLIGATION TO IMPROVE READING INSTRUCTION: On Overcoming Inertia and Staying ahead of the Courts

DANIEL M. SCHEMBER*

Millions of students in regular public school programs are not learning to read, while reports of reading programs in which previously unsuccessful students make dramatic gains remain either undisseminated or unconsidered. The findings of experimental programs, other special programs, and educational research are not being implemented, and the failing methods of the past are being perpetuated by inertia and indecision.

The law will not tolerate this situation much longer. Title I of the Elementary and Secondary Education Act of 1965 specifically requires its program planners to consider and, where appropriate, implement promising methodologies developed in demonstration projects or discovered through research.[1] "Right-to-education" lawsuits, moreover—both system-wide challenges raised in the context of school finance suits and individual "educational malpractice" litigation—are exposing the practices of schools in which children of normal intelligence do not learn. It is inevitable that remedies for inexcusable school failures will eventually be ordered.

While judicial intervention terminating unthinking continuation of the *status quo* is necessary and desirable, it will include painful consequences. The course of right-to-education litigation will be characterized (as it already is) by setbacks and advances over a protracted period of uncertainty. Uncertainty regarding the fundamental obligations of any institution has a debilitating impact on effectiveness.

The schools should avoid this uncertainty. Policy makers should not wait for lengthy litigation and court-ordered change. Rather, the trends of the law

---

*Daniel M. Schember is an attorney at law with Gaffney, Anspach, Schember, Klimaski, and Marks, PC.

should be anticipated. Legislation, establishing decision-making processes in education that will systematically address the problem of school failures, should be enacted. Such legislation, properly drawn, would preempt judicial intervention and effect orderly change.

Specifically, new legislation should establish procedures to detect reading failures, diagnose reading needs, implement responsive instructional strategies formulated in light of the results of research and the methods of successful reading programs, ensure that instructional staff are trained to implement the strategies chosen, and evaluate the effectiveness of reading programs to determine not just the extent to which they are failing or succeeding, but the reasons why—and the steps that might be taken to promote improvement.

In short, the schools should undertake the task of intelligent, continuous self-examination and assume the obligation to experiment.[2] The results of educational research, if they say nothing else, firmly establish that preserving the *status quo* risks error as equally as does implementation of several possible changes.

This discussion identifies no particular "equal risk" changes. Rather, the evidence of the existence of alternatives is sufficient to warrant new state legislation requiring educators to systematically consider that evidence, to reach their own conclusions, and, most important, to act on them. New legislation is needed not just to ensure that this process takes place, but also to protect educators from liability in making these efforts and to ensure that the process is implemented in an orderly way.[3] The logic of current legal developments already requires experimentation, but if those developments are simply allowed to take their course, change will arrive piecemeal, interspersed with periods of needless uncertainty.

### Student Illiteracy

A study of functional literacy by Louis Harris and Associates in 1970 estimated that 25 million persons in the United States "did not have the necessary skills for survival in our society. . . . Over seven million [of these persons] were under sixteen years of age."[4] In 1973, the National Foundation for the Improvement of Education cited studies indicating "that forty percent of the [urban] school population have severe reading difficulties and that the average grade level of achievement is no higher than fifth grade upon graduation."[5]

A study by the University of Texas conducted in the period from 1971 to 1975 echoed the Harris survey, finding 23 million members of the adult population "functionally incompetent" and only 46 percent of all adults "possessing the skills needed to cope with the complexities of modern living."[6]

### Successful Reading Programs and Educational Research Findings

Discussion of the ability of educational programs to improve the achievement of students who have not succeeded in the past has, in recent years, centered on evaluations of ESEA Title I programs. Title I, the largest federal education program, provides funds to meet the "special educational needs of educationally deprived children" in low income areas.[7]

Though initial studies were discouraging, there is now considerable evidence that Title I programs are producing significant effects. In the wake of "three large scale evaluations which . . . concluded that Title I was not successful" and the pessimistic findings of the Coleman Report,[8] which essentially found that school achievement was more closely correlated with social conditions than with differences in school resources or other school factors, the Department of Health, Education and Welfare (HEW) nonetheless was able to report the following in 1972:

> Expert experience suggests that .7 grade equivalent per year is usually the *most* which disadvantaged children gain in one year of school. But in many of the compensatory education programs we discuss, a sizeable proportion (often a majority) of the poor children tested seem to be achieving at a greater rate than this; while a smaller but still significant percentage are achieving at or above the national norm (1.0 grade equivalent gain per year).[9]

The HEW report also observed:

> The evidence available to us concerning specific Title I projects . . . demonstrates that successful compensatory education in settings of urban poverty poses a more difficult but not an impossible challenge. For example, among the more than twenty successful compensatory education projects identified by a research effort which sought to discover exemplary programs, many were inner-city efforts enrolling large proportions of disadvantaged and minority children.[10]

Subsequent analyses of the Coleman data[11] have produced conclusions contrary to those of the original Coleman Report and have placed the Coleman study in a fuller context. The early studies of Title I, moreover, were found to have two major defects. First, the evaluation techniques used were inadequate and, second, the programs evaluated simply did not implement the original concept of Title I as a program of concentrated expenditures to meet special needs for instruction and for other services.

By 1975, though, many Title I programs were operating in accordance with the intent of the law, several of the defects in evaluations of programs had been corrected, and the Office of Education was able to report:

> There are two main reasons why the debate about the achievement benefits of students who participate in basic skills projects funded by Title I appears to be diminishing. First, the incidence of successful projects is increasing to a point where their effect is beginning to appear in the aggregate. For example, evidence from state and national level Title I evaluations indicates

that project participants achieve at a rate that is equal to or greater than the national average while they are in the project. Second, a better understanding is developing of the general issues involved in evaluation and means are being devised to institute improved evaluation practices.[12]

Some studies have identified specific program factors that are consistently related to the reading gains of children in Title I programs. These factors include teacher experience, individualized instruction, the availability of immediate feedback to the pupil, tightly structured and carefully sequenced learning activities, clearly formulated program objectives and implementation of "time tested principles of management and organization." Some studies do not support these findings.[13] Furthermore, the problems of isolating and identifying relevant factors and of replicating initially successful programs remain unresolved. Nonetheless, two conclusions have emerged. First, different strategies work with different students. To optimize chances for success, teachers need to master a variety of techniques and acquire the ability both to perceive the circumstances under which alternative approaches are likely to work and to successfully apply each approach in that context. Second, each school and school district must actively develop the capacity to evaluate its own performance and respond to those evaluation findings. The uncertainties associated with replicating research results suggest that districts cannot wait for others to find "the one best way" and then simply adopt the method. The reality of successes demonstrated elsewhere, on the other hand, indicates that active local efforts to improve educational programs through careful planning, evaluation, and experimentation do obtain results.

### The Failure to Implement Research Findings

This kind of effort, however, is generally not being expended. Two recent studies of Title I found a virtual absence of systematic consideration and implementation of research findings by local school districts. The comptroller general's recent report on Title I found no school districts and only three states (of fourteen surveyed) that have "formal systems for disseminating information on exemplary projects."[14] A majority of the states indicated that they had received "insufficient information and training from [the Office of Education]" concerning information dissemination.[15] Another study reported that

> The major problem LEAs [local education agencies] have been having in planning Title I programs is that they "have not been exposed to new ideas and if they are exposed, they don't have time and resources to "pull off" new concepts . . . most of the states do not have policies ensuring that research information will be systematically disseminated to program planners.[16]

The absence of procedures for the consideration and implementation of research results in designing Title I programs strongly suggests that such procedures are also not employed when special state-funded programs and regular school programs are designed.

State laws, in fact, do not require such efforts. The most significant state reading law passed to date is California's Miller-Unruh Basic Reading Act of 1965.[17] Its express legislative intent is to provide "high quality" reading programs, but the act expressly forbids the state from disapproving district grant applications "on the basis of the methodology of providing basic reading instruction . . . which the school district has selected."[18] The act also establishes no requirement that districts attempt to determine the most suitable teaching methodologies. Ironically, the act nonetheless hypothesizes that such methods exist since it requires teachers designated for the program to pass a

> written examination . . . concerning . . . approaches and techniques which have been determined by competent authority to be most effective in imparting reading instruction . . . and concerning the appropriate selection of various techniques to meet the requirements of different pupils.[19]

In other states, the most significant legislation affecting reading instruction takes the form of recent accountability statutes enacted for the purpose of improving educational practices. Most of these laws, however, do not require educators to actually make a decision as to whether changes in instructional methodologies should be made. Some do not even require that changes be considered. Typically, these laws require only efforts to determine the extent to which achievement gains have been made without accompanying analysis of the reasons for success or failure.[20]

There are, however, some notable exceptions. The most significant of these is the accountability legislation in New Jersey, which requires the formulation of objectives and minimum proficiency standards, and, most important, a plan of "corrective action" in any case where those ends are not met.[21]

The special significance of the New Jersey legislation, however, is that it is a direct response to recent developments in a larger state-law context, a context which is being increasingly shaped by judicial intervention.

## The State Law Context

In addition to reading laws and accountability statutes, other sources of state law affect the teaching of reading, particularly the failure of the "normal" reading program to meet the needs of some students and the failure of the school to adapt the program to serve those students more effectively.

One recent court case sought to attach liability for this failure under a theory of educational malpractice.[22] It did not succeed, primarily because under the common law (or law created by courts and derived from Anglo-American legal traditions rather than official enactments) the failure to implement sound improvements in instructional strategies, and, indeed, the failure to adjust the "normal" program to serve those who do not benefit from it does not constitute professional negligence or educational malpractice by teachers, because teachers are obliged only to meet existing standards of practice; hence, neglect by all insulates each from liability.[23]

Failure to make efforts reasonably calculated to improve the capabilities of teachers probably does, however, contravene the requirements of some state inservice training statutes. One typical provision requires a county superintendent "to call conferences" and "in every way seek to foster in teachers professional insight and efficiency."[24]

The most important legal developments affecting reading instruction, however, are the implications of right-to-education litigation under the education clauses of state constitutions. The landmark case in this field is *Robinson* v. *Cahill*.[25] In *Robinson*, the New Jersey Supreme Court found that the state legislature failed to meet its constitutional obligation to define and establish a "thorough and efficient" education system to meet the educational needs of all students. The outgrowth of this decision was the accountability legislation mentioned earlier, which also incorporated teacher inservice training as a remedy for schools' failures to meet performance goals. Thus, this statute linked the usual assessment mechanisms of accountability statutes with inservice training statutes designed to promote improved teacher competence, and linked both of these to specific student performance objectives and state mechanisms designed to enforce the constitutional obligation. The formulation of plans for corrective action under this legislation will necessarily involve the active consideration and deliberate selection of alternative strategies for the teaching of reading.

## Implications of Current Legal Developments

Right-to-education litigation such as *Robinson* will require system-wide changes, including deliberate emphasis on both inservice training to improve the competence of teachers and the active consideration of alternative teaching strategies. This system-wide change will proceed slowly through the courts; major litigation always does.

Litigation under inservice training statutes might, in the meantime, force narrower efforts to improve teaching competencies. Also, the improvement of some teachers' abilities through mandatory use of research results stemming from Title I investigations will set new standards of accepted practice, destroying the "safety in numbers" effect which currently protects teachers from malpractice liability. Teachers who do not keep up will face a climate of increasing legal insecurity. This trend, however, will be a process characterized by sporadic developments, setbacks and advances, and other characteristic vagaries of litigation.

Rather than requiring teachers and administrators to endure the discomforting effects of piecemeal change, a more appropriate response is educational anticipation of the trend of law. New evidence concerning the efficacy of alternative teaching strategies should be systematically assimilated by a process of local decision making. New state legislation should require schools to assess their needs for reading instruction, diagnose problems, evaluate current practices, regularly consider new research evidence, make decisions concerning the courses of action most likely to succeed, train personnel to implement the chosen strategies, and, finally, put the strategies and training to work in actual practice. These are elementary steps necessary to bring rationality to educational policy making at the local level and to enable failing school systems to begin to pull themselves out of a malaise of ineffectiveness, inertia and indecision.

## Notes

1. Section 141 (a) (10); 20 U.S.C.S., Section 241e (a).

2. Daniel P. Moynihan and Frederick Mosteller, eds., "On Equality of Educational Opportunity," in Constantine Menges et al., *The Effectiveness of Compensatory Education: Summary and Review of the Evidence* (Washington, D.C.: Department of Health, Education and Welfare, Office of Program Planning and Evaluation, 1972). [ED 062 475]

3. The reference here is to malpractice liability. For discussion of the general standard applicable in this regard see the text at note 21.

4. Louis Harris and Associates, *Survival Literacy Study* (New York: Louis Harris and Associates, Inc., 1976). [ED 068 813]

5. National Foundation for the Improvement of Education, *The Improvement of Literacy*, 1973.

6. John Matthews, "Twenty-three Million of Us Are 'Functionally Incompetent,'" *Washington Star* 29 October, 1975.

7. 20 U.S.C. Section 241 (a) *et seq*.

8. James S. Coleman et al., *Equality of Educational Opportunity* (Washington, D.C.: Department of Health, Education and Welfare, National Center for Educational Statistics), 1966. [ED 012 275]

9. Menges, *Effectiveness of Compensatory Education*, pp. 7-8.

10. *Ibid*.

11. See Eric Hanushek, "The Education of Negroes and Whites" (Ph.D. diss., Massachusetts Institute of Technology, 1968), as reported in Herbert J. Kiesling, *Educational Productivity: Public Concern and Legislative Response* (Washington, D.C.: National Conference of State Legislatures, 1975). [ED 112 517]

12. U.S., Department of Health, Education and Welfare, Office of Education, *Annual Evaluation Report on Programs Administered by the U.S. Office of Education, Fiscal Year 1975*, p. 86. [ED 125 109]

13. Kiesling, *Educational Productivity*.

14. Comptroller General of the U.S., *Assessment of Reading Activities under the Federal Program of Aid for Educationally Deprived Children. Report to Congress* (Washington, D.C.: Department of Health, Education and Welfare, Office of Education, 1975), p. 32. [ED 116 171]

15. *Ibid*.

16. Lawyers' Committee for Civil Rights Under Law, *An Analysis of the Basis for, and Clarity and Restrictiveness of, the Program Requirements Applicable to Local School Districts Applying for Grants under Title I of the Elementary and Secondary Education Act of 1965*, 1977), p. 323.

17. California Education Code, Section 5770 *et seq*. (West 1975).

18. California Education Code, Section 5790.

19. California Education Code, Section 5776.

20. Phyllis Hawthorne, *Legislation by the States: Accountability and Assessment in Education* rev. (Madison, Wisc.: Cooperative Accountability Project, Wisconsin State Department of Public Instruction, 1973). [ED 078 513]

21. New Jersey S.B. 1516, Section 15.

22. *Peter Doe* v. *San Francisco Unified School District*, Civil No. 36851 1st District Ct. App. (1975).

23. For a general discussion of this case, see "Comment: Educational Malpractice," *University of Pennsylvania Law Review* 124 (1976): 755-56.

24. 52 Education Code of Alabama, Section 115 (1975).

25. 62 N.J. 473 (1973).

# THE CHANGING THEORY OF THE READING PROCESS: Does Society Really Know How It Reads?

ROBERT J. HARPER II
GARY KILARR*

The preceding papers in this volume raise our consciousnesses to the complexity of issues brought about by new laws that affect reading achievement and instruction. To extend our understanding of these issues and to gain better insight into this complexity, an examination of the currently changing view of reading is necessary. What we will assert is that new knowledge suggests a different theory of reading that may be more appropriate than the traditional view.

At the same time, a historical event is used to draw a parallel that exemplifies the current unrest in our society over education and basic skills, the outcome of which unrest may prevent the utilization of this new knowledge through crippling legislation. Issues are clouded because, in reality, what is occurring is society's reaction to changing values. The complexity of the issues involved is further amplified through the use and interpretation of standardized tests. While not inappropriate for some purposes, these tests are totally inappropriate for evaluating reading.

The development of this new theory and its translation into classroom practice requires teacher decision making based on the understanding of this fact. We are led to the conclusion that reasonable solutions can only be attained when both citizens and public institutions, as well as policy makers, are knowledgeable of the basic theory of reading and reading instruction.

While we consider these complexities as parameters of the problem, we must point out that reaction to change itself may be our major challenge.

*Robert J. Harper II is a policy analyst for the Lawyer's Committee for Civil Rights Under Law, Washington, D.C. Gary Kilarr is an assistant professor at Virginia Polytechnic Institute and State University.

When a new theory or point of view evolves, currently held notions are perceived by many to be directly challenged. As a result, conditions of unrest and dissatisfaction are often prevalent. This is not to say that the new theory is causing the unrest; on the contrary, the new theory usually attempt to provide a solution to an existing state of unrest and dissatisfaction. New theories are, in fact, stimulated as traditional ways of thinking fail to answer questions and provide guidance.

Unfortunately, a new theory can be rejected out of hand, become a scapegoat for the unrest, or be overlooked. The authorities may pass new laws, rules, and regulations, usually unfavorable to the new theory and favorable to reviving past conditions and attitudes. Such acts attempt to strengthen what the authorities perceive as a weakening and deteriorating society; at the same time, the authorities' vested interests are maintained. These laws are an attempt to return the society to the traditional way of doing things, a return to the "basics" of the apparently more desirable past.

The current effort to return to the basics of reading instruction reflected by recent legislative actions in many states is an example of such an attempt to quell a society that is, in this case, restless and concerned about education. Apparently, what has previously been regarded as an adequate theory of reading is not providing the guidance and answers necessary to explain why many children cannot read. To fully understand the relationship between reading failure and the current state of unrest in education, particularly as it affects reading instruction, a short venture into history may offer an illustrative parallel.

In *The Ascent of Man*, J. Bronowski describes the growth and development of early civilization as dependent upon humans making sense of the stars, the moon, and the sun.[1] Knowledge of astronomy provided opportunities to develop theories from which interpretations and predictions relating to the seasons, calendar, and travel could be derived. Travel, in particular, was a major contributor to the growth of civilization. One could easily use geographic features and trail-markers on land, but for sea travel, another strategy was necessary. The civilization that could best make sense of the world, all other things being equal, flourished. Making sense, however, was not automatic, took time, and gave rise to conflict.

In the 16th century, a new theory began to challenge traditional views of the world. At that time, the traditional view of the motion of the planets and the sun was based on the Ptolemaic theory, which had proved to be useful for over a thousand years and, so it would seem, was likely to continue as a source of guidance. Ptolemy stated that the earth was the center about which all the stars, planets, and the sun traveled. Elaborate explanations of the known universe, with the earth as the center, were written; even mechanical models of this marvelous complexity were constructed. The geocentric concept of the world was the order of the day. Columbus made his historic voyage by applying the Ptolemaic view of the world. Clearly, the theory was sound, but the complexity of the theory suggested further investigation. Was there a simpler, or clearer, explanation?

In 1543, Nicholas Copernicus postulated a hypothesis conceptualizing a simpler sense of the heavens in *De Revolutionibus Orbium Coelestrium*. In this small volume, the sun was described as the center around which the planets traveled—a heliocentric view, and a simple idea that provided a better explanation of the observed phenomenon in the heavens. A new theory of the world had begun to emerge. The full impact of its emergence did not occur until later, when Galileo developed his systems of scientific observation. With the aid of a new invention, the telescope, Galileo was able to observe the heavens in a way that had never before been possible. The recordings of his discoveries, when published in 1610, revealed for the first time "that the Ptolemaic heavens simply would not work. Copernicus' powerful guess had been right and now stood open and revealed."[2]

The seeds of controversy sown earlier by Copernicus had been cultivated by Galileo in a society already torn apart by the Reformation and the Counter-Reformation. Galileo struggled to find support for the Copernican view from the authority of the day—the Catholic church. But, in 1616, the Church prohibited the holding, teaching, and support of the heliocentric sense of the world. Laws, rules, and regulations were developed to protect the society and return it to a traditional view.

Galileo continued quietly to establish support for the Copernican theory and published the *Dialogue on the Great World Systems* in 1632. Within the next year, Galileo was tried by the Inquisition, recanted his belief in the heliocentric theory, and remained under house arrest until his death in 1642. The Copernican theory, as supported by the evidence Galileo had collected, was too much for the authorities to cope with in relationship to the political events of the times.

The theory challenged the very nature of belief and insulted humankind's concept of itself as the center of life and the world. The theory became a political question and, in the political upheaval of the time, was a casualty. Of course, the real casualty was the system of authority, for as it sought to maintain its equilibrium by denying the existence of an idea through laws, rules, and regulations, the tide of reasoned evidence overwhelmed it.

Currently, legislatures, courts, and school boards have found themselves in a similar situation. Reinforced by educators who have long believed that they had the capability, and schools the capacity, to produce a literate society, the authorities of our schools are daily articulating policies demanding accountability, competency-based graduation standards, and rigid performance objectives for various age and grade levels.[3] Although it is undoubtedly within the purview of the schools to make every effort to meet those standards, for most schools, "every effort" translates into "more of the same."

Questioning the assumptions and beliefs upon which the schools operate does not formally take place, nor is it encouraged.

The focus of these activities has been on the language arts in the form of a back-to-basics movement. These actions, designed to provide better reading, writing, and arithmetic instruction for the consumer public, can hardly be unexpected. However, isn't the treatment of this concern through laws, rules, and regulations superficial? Parents, teachers, reading specialists, college professors of reading, lawyers, and legislators can and do make decisions about a reader's competence. These decisions are based on their understanding of what makes a competent reader and can be classified into categories that represent distinctly different and conflicting views of reading competence. Particularly in reading instruction, one must ask if laws are not being passed on the basis of a theory of reading that is outdated.

These varying views are often the basis for conflict and confusion for not only the parent and teacher, but for the learner as well. Which view is correct? Given the current state of reading research, this question may not be answerable, but a discussion of these views may provide insights in clarifying the reading process. Instructional practices and research in reading suggest that there are two current views of reading. The first view states that reading is an exact process, the second, that reading is not an exact process. These two views can be compared by looking at how a reader's performance is judged by them.

A boy of ten was asked to read an unfamiliar story orally. When he interpreted the text differently than was expected, notations were made. The results of reading the first hundred words of the story are given below, with the addition of three other sentences from the reading.

THE LINE DOWN THE MIDDLE OF THE ROOM[4]

1. Victor and Billy were brothers.

2. "Look what you did!" said Victor to

3. Billy one day. "You broke my plane!"

4. "I didn't mean to," Billy said.

5. Victor picked up his broken plane. "I

6. told you not to get into my things," he

7. said. (uc) 2. went / 1. won't

8. "I just wanted to see it," Billy said.

9. "This was my new plane!" Victor said.

10. He took Billy by the arm. "Say you're
    (c) 2. my / 1. and

11. sorry."

12. "You can't make me say ~~anything~~," said
    *nothing*

13. Billy.

———————————

14. Victor took something out of his pocket.

15. "See this ~~role~~ of tape?" he said. "I'm
    *paper*

16. going to put a line of tape right down the
    *paper*

17. ~~middle~~ of the room!"
    *mittle*

18. When Victor got into bed that night, he
    (uc) 2. Vittor / 1. your     *whot*

19. forgot to turn off the light.
    (c) 2. begot / 1. befor     (c) 2. cut / 1. si —

———————————

20. "But I can't pick the papers up," he

21. said.

———————————

22. He got out of bed and pulled the tape (A)

23. off the floor.

What does this information suggest as to the competence of the reader? According to the view of reading as an exact process, the reader is expected to read everything accurately, as printed on the page, in order to understand the message of the author.[5] Any deviation from the exact reading is considered an error. Errors that occur are diagnosed to determine the help a reader needs.[6] Did the reader pronounce the word correctly? Was a word left out or inserted? Does the reader look only at the beginning of words? The endings? Such a diagnosis becomes the basis for subsequent instruction.

The reader may be instructed to sound out an unknown word using phonetic analysis skills. Daily drill on other basic skills such as word order, syllabication, and vowel blends is provided as reinforcement to establish mastery of previously learned skills.

With this view of reading as an exact process in mind, an examination of a few of the errors that our reader made would lead us to conclude that instruction is necessary to help the reader with pronunciation, reversals, substitutions, function words, and sound/letter relationships. For example, errors in pronunciation include *Vittor* for *Victor, mittle* for *middle*, and *din't* for *didn't*. Reversals are apparent for *Billy said* and *But I can't pick the papers up* and suggest that more careful reading is necessary for this individual. Substitutions are also inexact duplications of the print, as exemplified by *paper* for *tape* and *nothing* for *anything*. These are just a few of the many errors made by this reader that would be perceived by a proponent of this view of reading.

Depending on the criteria used for evaluation, this reader made from nine to sixteen errors per hundred words. This reader would be viewed, therefore, as making too many errors to be regarded as reading with an acceptable degree of comprehension.

Viewed from the perspective of the letter and word, the model of reading becomes a world in which satellites of skill categories revolve: vocabulary, speed of reading, reading comprehension, blending and recognizing syllables, sound discrimination, perceptual forms, word recognition, skimming, fixations, regressions, average spans of recognition, directional attack, letter identification, simple consonents and combinations, short vowel sounds, visual copying, visual-perception memory for words, visual-perception memory in association and kinesthetic memory, logical thinking, word study skills, paragraph meaning, using an index, recognizing commas, abbreviations, motor integration, and physical development. All of these skills or characteristics center on the word or letter—how to recognize it, how to attack it, how to know its meaning. A word/letter-centered theory of reading and instruction is complicated, complex, and abstract and has become, to many, an article of faith. It has become a way of viewing and teaching reading that represents a tradition moving back to the basics.

Another view of reading competence asserts that reading is not an exact process; this is a view of reading that has been emerging from the literature on reading. It is a process in which the reader is actively engaged in a search for meaning from the printed page by selecting information (not all information), using hypotheses (guessing), and testing and modifying.[7] The reader will indicate his or her active processing of the author's message by deviations (errors) from what is actually printed. These deviations are not considered errors, but are called miscues.

Miscues are analyzed to assess the strengths and weaknesses of the reader's processing of language. Miscues are considered indicators of strengths when language and meaning are kept intact. Conversely, miscues that do not keep language and meaning intact are indicators of weakness. For example, a child was asked to reading the following sentence: "Then he saw the tree and all of the waiting people." However, the child read, "Then he saw the tree and all *the people were waiting*." The meaning of the sentence appears changed, but not changed significantly when judged in terms of the author's intended meaning within the total context. The reader also reconstructed the original sentence into another perfectly acceptable English sentence. In order to do this, the reader must have had some idea of the author's message.

With the view in mind of reading as an inexact process, an examination of the same selected errors our reader made, as noted above, would bring us to conclude that a different instructional focus may be necessary. This reader's pronunciation represents dialect differences that all readers exhibit and that do not interfere with meaning. The reversal of a dialogue carrier makes no change in meaning. The substitution of *nothing* for *anything* (line 12) is fully acceptable in terms of meaning. The use of *paper* for *tape* (line 15) is acceptable to convey the intention that the room be divided. It is interesting to note that the last time the author used the word *tape* (line 22), the reader said *tape*.

The substitution of *cut* for *turn* (line 19) is probably the greatest indicator of the reader's strength. This reader's dialect community says "cut off the lights" rather than "turn off the lights." The reader's reproduction of the word *cut* instead of *turn* indicates that the reader must be aware of *lights* at the end of the phrase and at the same time aware of the meaning the author intended. We can also conclude that this material was understood by the reader.[8] There is a strong suggestion here that no special instruction is necessary.

The emerging meaning-centered theory of reading provides a different model. Its satellites are strategies which promote reading for meaning—guessing, trying, discarding, and guessing again until sense is reached—the same techniques used in problem solving. Skill satellites involve language, language experience, language clarification, and learning to use language to convey meaning. Other satellites involve knowledge, knowledge acquisition, knowledge assimilation, and knowledge application. Additional skills relate to using words in context, guessing the meaning that makes sense, discarding a meaningless guess, and substituting another guess. More skill satellites involve the construction of a graphophonemic system based on the language already known that makes sense to the individual reader, a system designed to gain meaning, rather than to be the center upon which all else focuses.

Thus, we have two conflicting theories of reading, analogous to the past conflict of astronomical theories—the traditional, dominant view of reading as an exact process (letter and word-centered), like the Ptolemaic view of the world; and the newer, challenging view that reading is not an exact process (meaning-centered), like the Copernican view.

Copernicus decided that the complex universe could be explained with simple clarifying statements that were based on a theoretical change in perspective. Changing one's perspective of how reading works also requires a theoretical change. Reading viewed as a language process with the focus on meaning may be the change in perspective necessary for improvement of reading instruction; new knowledge will eventually help us to decide the most appropriate path.

The court, legislative, and policy decisions that are based on a less knowledgeable notion of how reading works are playing a pronounced role in determining schools' reading programs. These events are beginning to place restrictions that require the use of questionable instructional practices. Reading has become a political issue, and the return to "basics" has become a salve for public concern about the graduation of students who cannot effectively read or write. The danger of this turn of events is that these laws, rules, and regulations will cause educators to ignore new knowledge and will present even greater obstacles to the improvement of instruction. Whether or not the emerging meaning-centered theory of reading is better than the traditional view is not the most important issue; that new knowledge may be outlawed is our concern.

A new understanding or theory of reading is not enough to establish a viable policy for our schools. Inextricably linked with any theory of reading is the process through which the reading program will be evaluated. Standardized norm-referenced reading tests are powerful authorities in today's education, as demonstrated by periodic reports of test results by the news media. With few exceptions, the emphasis is on low test scores, and, to the public, low scores mean unequivocally poor schools. The present use and construction of standardized tests to measure reading ability needs to be reconsidered in light of the changing theory of the reading process. Two major problems exist with regard to the use of standardized tests: the construction of tests that discriminate ability and the misuse of tests.

When test developers decide to create a test to measure skills, they first set up objectives in each content and skill area that the test will cover. This is accomplished through analysis of current textbooks and curriculum guides and through consideration of the advice of experts. Having decided the objectives that will be tested, designers then write questions to test these objectives and, more importantly, to discriminate between those taking the test. These items are then put into test form and tried out on sample schools that are representative of the national school population.

The "try out" test results are then analyzed and each item is evaluated for inclusion in the final test. As test designers want their test to discriminate between good and poor mastery of skills, the final items must meet certain criteria when judged as a whole. All the questions measuring a skill must result in scores that spread out along a range and, at the same time, tend to group up around the average score. Items are selected which consistently fall in the upper or lower ranges of difficulty; students who can answer a question should consistently be within a certain range. Items are also judged as to whether the average scores of older groups are higher than those of younger groups. Items that do not discriminate between groups are rejected. The job of the test developer is, then, to construct items that discriminate.

It is more feasible to build a test that discriminates between groups if the view of reading upon which the test is based is word/letter-centered and if comprehension is measured according to what the test maker decides is the best answer. On the other hand, it is improbable that a standardized reading test can be derived from the meaning-centered view of reading. (There presently exists no test that views reading as meaning-centered.)

Once the item-analysis is done, the test is complete. It now must be normed so that scores can be compared and discriminations made. In norming a test, developers select a sample of students, stratified by community size and socioeconomic characteristics, that represents the national student population. Racial and ethnic representativeness is usually assured. The test is given to a large sample—approximately 20,000 students per grade. All scores for each grade level or age level are then plotted, the range of scores and the average score are determined, and the corresponding percentile that each score represents is calculated.

Further importance is given to the average score by the development of grade-equivalent scores.[9] In order to obtain grade-equivalent scores, each grade-level test is given to samples of students in other grades. For instance, the fourth-grade battery is given to third graders and fifth graders. The average scores of the third graders, fourth graders, and fifth graders are calculated. Average scores obtained by this procedure provide the basis for grade-equivalent scores. A fourth grader who obtains a grade-equivalent score of 5.0, for example, has an average score that is the same as a fifth grader who took the fourth-grade test. The score does not indicate that the fourth grader would have an average score on the fifth-grade test. Once these scores have been established for the norming sample, the test is then standardized.[10]

When students take a standardized test, the score is compared to the score of the average groups and is reported as a grade-equivalent score, a percentile score, or some other such comparative measure. The use of this score comparison, while not the fault of the test creators, is another indication of lack of knowledge concerning test construction and use.

A state policy requiring students to read, for example, at a sixth-grade level in order to receive a certificate of promotion or to graduage from high school, while admirable in the eyes of the public, is based on the false notion that there is a specific sixth-grade reading level. There are, however, such labels as *grade-equivalent scores*. Although these labels should not be interpreted as reading levels, unfortunately, they too often are.

The lack of understanding of the meaning of grade-equivalent scores is a major basis for the false notion that there is a reading level for each grade. That this false notion is held by a majority can be consistently demonstrated by asking individuals what a particular grade-equivalent score reflects: a very high percentage of the time, the answer will be that it is the reading grade level for that child. Further questioning will reveal that the grade-equivalent score is the most singly used determinant in selecting reading materials; that is, a reader with a grade-equivalent score of 2.0 is frequently given reading material with a readability measure of 2.0, or that most often found in second-grade classrooms. This current, inappropriate use of grade-equivalent scores for reading placement is evidence of a general lack of understanding about the value and use of a test.[11] Many educators, legislatures, and courts, however, continue to operate on this notion. To question the acceptance of these test results seems not to be a concern.

If we are to accept these tests as a measure of student competence in reading, there are several questions that must be answered. The first is, What does a score mean? If the test has been carefully constructed (and most norm-referenced tests are), we can say a student's score is greatly below the average, below the average, average, above average, or greatly above average. We cannot say why the student scored the way he or she did. We cannot analyze strengths and weaknesses in reading. We probably cannot say if the particular student will or will not be a good reader as an adult. The test tells us little about the person taking it. The authority of the test rests in the fact that it gives a number designed not to measure reading skills, but to discriminate between reading skills that will compare a child to an average reader in that test's norming sample. The purpose of a "discriminating" test item is important for us to consider, for it often requires the test creator to distort the subject matter being tested. For the discrimination process to be used in making a standardized reading test, reading must be regarded as an exact process. One cannot discriminate between average or below average readers without using questions that reflect a view of reading that fragments the ability to read into small mastery units. These units then become the ends, and the meaning is lost.

This leads us to our second question: Are the skills measured by standardized tests really a measure of reading? Reading skills are measured in early grades by testing word-attack skills and ability to decode or recode. It is predictable, given the emphasis on basic skills in federal and state dollars, that children will begin to score better on beginning reading tests. They will demonstrate that teachers are teaching, but will children really be reading?

In later grades, the tests of reading are composed of passages and questions to be answered about the passages. Again, the outcomes are predictable. Children taught in the lower grades to look at bits and pieces of language, with little or no focus on meaning, will do poorly. We will have another crisis in reading instruction. The use of such tests will continue to show that students are not necessarily learning to read. A continued use and belief in these tests will automatically lead teachers to recant the new evidence toward a meaning-centered theory of reading. This situation is tantamount to teachers being held in house arrest, like Galileo, in this case by the authority of tests that measure precision achieved through discrimination principles. Accumulating evidence leads us to believe that it is time to reject the existing theory of reading prevalent in today's schools and the tests which derive from it.

We have, then, two perspectives from which to view reading; one which focuses on parts of language, and the other which focuses on the whole meaning of language. The latter view has emerged as researchers have attempted to view reading in light of the relationship between thought and language. This research is having a revolutionary effect on what we know about reading.[12] It will soon be important to articulate both views clearly. The bits, fragments, and pieces present in the research must be sorted out. Thoughts need to be consolidated, stands taken, and the issues polarized by educators in order to establish a viable reading theory. There are too many people making decisions about reading who are not aware of the basis of their beliefs or of the existence of alternatives. There is an effort on the part of some to incorporate all perspectives of reading—an eclectic view, but conflicting theories lead us to practices that often are in opposition. (The Ptolemaic and Copernican theories are mutually exclusive.) Educators must investigate what views of reading exist and examine the reasons for them. They must realize that choices must be made between different perspectives and that these decisions must be justified to communities who are aware of the alternatives.

Schools are, indeed, responsible for the delivery of instruction in reading and the other language processes. They cannot shirk this responsibility by claiming that the socioeconomic levels of students determine their reading potential; that genetic factors predetermine abilities; or that the home and community environment overpowers the environment and resources of the schools.

The lack of leadership on the reading issues among educators is abhorrent and has resulted in schools that are run by the courts. What is needed is a new leadership in education and a restructuring of resources and beliefs to actively fulfill the promise of a functionally literate society.

Teacher trainers should address the conflicting theories of reading not superficially in terms of which is right or wrong, but critically, in recognition that teachers need a new set of strategies for rational decision making in order to make sense of the often conflicting findings of research, and with the knowledge that significant time and commitment are necessary to prepare teachers for the task.

Professional organizations must find ways to loosen their ties to vested interests in order to establish their proper role as a marketplace of ideas, as a place for challenging debate.

The time and attention necessary for teachers to know whether a student understands what he or she reads will necessitate reduced class sizes and the use of individualized instruction. Present standardized tests must be rejected and demands made for alternative evaluation instruments. Cultural, community, and environmental factors will not be roadblocks, but building blocks, for understanding and will necessitate a redirection of teaching to utilize the strengths of these factors.

Schools must commit their resources to these ends. Where problems occur, an active assessment must take place to create new strategies and to determine solutions. The scope of this process is all encompassing within the realm of the schools. A reallocation of educational resources may well be necessary to achieve these goals, and this process may have to be repeated many times before we have reached the limit of the schools' environment.

At that point, educators must focus their efforts as agents of change in the greater society to facilitate necessary new resources and strategies. Presently, this is not being accomplished. Educational leadership is by default. Courts and lawmakers are left with the responsibility for education and have become the active agents. A new commitment to the basis of our democratic process is necessary, a commitment to intelligent decision making, and reading is the key. As Thomas Jefferson noted:

> I know no safe depository of the ultimate powers of the society but the people themselves; and if we think them not enlightened enough to exercise their control with a wholesome discretion, the remedy is not to take it from them, but to inform their discretion.[13]

While the courts and the legislatures are taking an active role in the development of a national policy concerned with language processes, educators, for the most part, remain profoundly silent.

## Notes

1. For a more complete discussion, see Jacob Brownowski, *The Ascent of Man* (Boston/Toronto: Little, Brown & Company, 1973).

2. Brownowski, *The Ascent of Man*, p. 204.

3. Consult the appendix for a listing of policies.

4. From "The Line Down the Middle of the Room" by Joanne Oppenheim, exerpted with permission of Macmillan Publishing Co., Inc. from *Green Light, Go* (A Bank Street

Reader) by Bank Street College of Education. ©Copyright Macmillan Publishing Co., Inc. 1966, 1972.

5. N. J. Silvaroli, *Classroom Reading Inventory*, 2nd ed. (Dubuque, Iowa: William C. Brown Company, 1973), pp. 7-15.

6. D. Laberge and S. J. Samuels, "Toward a Theory of Automatic Information Processing in Reading," Cognitive Psychology 6 (1974): 293-323.

7. Kenneth S. Goodman, "Reading: A Psycholinguistic Guessing Game," *Journal of the Reading Specialist* 7(1967): 126-35; see also Kenneth S. Goodman and Carolyn L.Burke, *Theoretically Based Studies of Pattern of Miscues in Oral Reading Performance:* Final Report (Washington, D.C.: Department of Health, Education and Welfare, Office of Education, Bureau of Research, 1973), pp. 1-11.

8. The reader retold the story in his own words immediately after the exercise. The retelling indicated that he did, indeed, comprehend the material.

9. See L. F. Anderholter, *Major Misconceptions about Grade Equivalent Scores* (Bensenville, Ill.: Scholastic Testing, 1960).

10. This discussion of standarized test construction is brief and does not explain other elaborate procedures that are commonly and conscientiously employed by test makers.

11. See Lois E. Burrill, *How a Standardized Achievement Test is Built: Test Service Notebook No. 125* (New York: Harcourt, Brace, Jovanovich, n.d.).

12. See the *Harvard Education Review* 47 (1977), an entire issue devoted to reading, language, and learning.

13. Thomas Jefferson, in a letter to William Charles Jarvis.

# APPENDIX

The following compendium of state laws affecting reading instruction was developed after an extensive search of state education codes. Code provisions establish the basic legal framework for a state's education system, but the actual day-to-day functioning of a classroom teacher is much more affected by regulations and policies developed as a result of the codes. Unfortunately, the codification of the education regulations and policies seldom occurs. In addition, both regulations and policy statements change frequently, making it nearly impossible to keep up with these refinements in one state, much less fifty.

Therefore, a systematic and timely collection of all legal provisions—statutes, regulations, and policies—for all the states is not possible. Accordingly, our investigation has been limited to the latest education codes and supplements from each of the various states. Research for this compendium was originally done in August 1976 at the Library of Congress and was updated in August 1977 and January 1978.

The twenty-five descriptors (or subject terms) used in entering the codes were chosen by Hannah Geffert, research associate for the Lawyers' Committee for Civil Rights Under Law, after an analysis of a sample of state codes. It is feasible that statutory provisions may have been missed; however, these exceptions are limited.

Nonetheless, readers should not rely on this compilation to reflect all legal requirements in their own or other states. Interested parties should supplement this compendium by inquiring about state regulations and policies interpreting each statute at the appropriate state department of education or chief state school officer's headquarters. The accompanying code provisions do provide, as a whole, good examples of the various ways in which state legislatures are addressing the question of reading and language-arts requirements through legislation.

Acknowledgements for work performed on this compendium must be extended to Martha Rowland, Hannah Geffert, Cherie Root and Robert J. Harper.

---

ALABAMA

52:17     Courses of study

The state board of education, on the recommendation of the state superintendent of education, shall prescribe the minimum contents of courses of study for all public elementary and high schools in the state, and shall fix the maximum number of books which are compulsory in each grade of the elementary schools. In every elementary school in the state there shall be taught at least reading, spelling, handwriting, arithmetic, oral and written English, geography, history of the United States and Alabama, elementary science, hygiene and sanitation, physical training, and such other studies as may be prescribed by the state board of education. English shall be the only language employed in teaching of the first six grades of the elementary schools in the state (1927).

52:124     Institutes and reading circle work

The county superintendent of education shall organize and attend county and local institutes for teachers and citizens, and shall organize and direct the reading circle work of the county, advise teachers as to their further study in professional reading, and assist parents and citizens to acquire knowledge of the aims and work of the school. (1927 School Code, 162.)

52:408     Studies required to be taught in elementary school

In every elementary school in the state there shall be taught reading, spelling and writing, arithmetic, oral and written English, geography, history of the United States and Alabama, elementary science, hygiene and sanitation, physical training and such other studies as may be prescribed by the state board of education. English shall be the only language employed in teaching in the first six grades of the elementary schools in the state.

ARIZONA

15:1131    Testing pupils in elementary grades

A standardized reading achievement test adopted by the state board of education shall be given annually in the first week of October to all pupils who are enrolled in the third grade. A standardized mathematics achievement test adopted by the state board of education shall be given annually in the first week of October to all pupils who are enrolled in the fifth grade. The state board of education shall promulgate rules and regulations governing the methods for the administration of all such uniform tests.

15:1132    Testing pupils in grades higher than the third

The superintendent may require the pupils in grades higher than the third to take uniform tests of a nature similar to that required by this article for third grade pupils.

15:1133    Acceptable tests

Any test employed shall be uniform throughout the state. The tests shall be adopted for use by the state board of education, and shall be printed or purchased and distributed to the various school districts by the office of the state superintendent.

15:1134    Tests results

The results of any uniform tests administered to pupils under this article shall be reported to the state board of education. The results shall include the score of each individual pupil, the score of each classroom, the score of each school and such other information or comparative data as the state board of education may by regulation require. A copy of such results shall be retained in the office of the state superintendent. A copy of the results from each district shall be sent to the district. No results shall be otherwise released until ten days after the report to each district. The state superintendent, by utilizing experts in the field of test evaluations, shall annually assess the effectiveness of reading programs. An annual report shall be submitted to the state board of education, to the legislature, each district board of education in the state and all superintendents. The state board of education shall annually make recommendations to the legislature with respect to such test results and analysis which will enhance the quality of the reading program in the public schools.


# ARKANSAS

No code provisions found.


# CALIFORNIA

5770    Citation of act

This chapter may be cited as the Miller-Unruh Basic Reading Act of 1965.


5771    Statement of legislative intent and purpose

It is the intent and purpose of the Legislature that the elementary school reading program provided for by this chapter shall be directed to the prevention of reading disabilities, and the correction of reading disabilities at the earliest possible time in the educational career of the pupil. The instruction program shall be provided in grades 1, 2, and 3 in the elementary schools. The instruction program may be provided in kindergarten if the governing board of a school district, by resolution, acts to make the program so applicable. With respect to any district in which the instructional program has been made applicable to kindergarten, the units of average daily attendance in kindergarten shall in no manner be utilized in the computation of the basic quota of specialist reading teachers, computation of allowances for specialist reading teachers, establishment of a system of priorities, or computation for the salary allotment for professional school librarians, nor shall any kindergarten teachers be eligible to apply for a scholarship grant for teachers of reading. It is the intent of the Legislature that the applicability of the instructional program to kindergarten shall in no manner affect the school districts' entitlements for the program authorized by this chapter or shall in no manner affect the statewide priorities established with respect to the program authorized by this chapter.

It is the further intent of the Legislature that the reading program in the public schools be of high quality, and that the program be designed to permit early development of reading skills, and the early correction of reading disabilities. The Legislature recognized that early development of reading ability enhances the opportunity of each pupil for success in school and for success in a career upon leaving school. The Legislature further recognizes that to achieve its intent and purpose it will be necessary to provide means to employ teachers trained in the teaching of reading, to provide incentives to encourage such training, and to stimulate the establishment and maintenance of school libraries. To carry out its intent and purpose, the Legislature has enacted this chapter to provide salary payments for specialist teachers in reading, scholarships to encourage the development of skills in the teaching of reading, and salary payments for the employment of professional librarians in school districts. It is also the intent of the Legislature that the provisions, of this chapter shall be administered to provide funds and services first to those school districts and to the schools in such districts where the need for reading instruction is greatest and the financial ability of the district to provide it is least. This program is voluntary and any school district may participate or may decline to participate. If a district participates, it shall participate fully with respect to those schools in the district in which the program is established.

5771.1   Request for participation on reduced basis, requirements

During the 1966-67 school year, and thereafter, if a school district is unable to participate fully in the reading program established under this chapter on a school or district basis because of its inability to employ enough specialist teachers to fully meet the basic quota of certificated employees to be appointed specialist teachers as provided in Section 5781 and 5782, the governing board of the district may request approval of the State Superintendent of Public Instruction for participation in the program on a reduced basis. Such approval may be granted by the State Superintendent of Public Instruction if he determines that:

(a) In districts having more than one school, all reasonable efforts are made to concentrate available teachers in the school or schools where the need for the program is the greatest so that such schools may benefit from full participation in the program so far as possible.

(b) For the 1966-67 school year, the applicant district or school employs at least 30 percent of the basic quota of certificated employees to be appointed specialist teachers as computed under the provisions of Section 5781 and 5782.

(c) For the 1967-68 school year, and thereafter, the applicant district or school employs at least 30 percent of the basic quota of certificated employees to be appointed specialist teachers as computed under the provisions of Section 5781 and 5782.

5772    State Board of Education to adopt rules and regulations

The State Board of Education shall have the power to adopt and promulgate rules and regulations necessary to the effective administration of this chapter, including but nor necessary limited to those specifically required to be adopted by particular provisions of this chapter.

5773    Definitions as used in this chapter:

(a) "Specialist teacher" shall mean a person holding a credential as a specialist teacher in reading, issued by the Commission for Teacher Preparation and Licensing, and employed by a school district for the duties listed in Section 5785.

(b) "Average daily attendance" shall, except as otherwise specifically provided, mean average daily attendance during the preceding fiscal year.

5774    School district governing board authorized to participate in federal programs

The governing board of any school district is authorized to accept the provisions of any act of Congress under which federal funds are available for purposes of this chapter, and may participate in any program provided thereunder in order to accept and expand such federal funds to such act of Congress and this chapter. Participation may include the expenditure by the school district of whatever funds may be required by the federal government as a condition to such participation.

5774.1    Appointment of specialist teacher, consolidated application form, request for federal funds

The State Board of Education shall prepare a consolidated application form for use by each school district making application for appointment of a specialist teacher. The consolidated application form shall include any request for funds under Titles I, II, and III of the Elementary and Secondary Education Act of 1965, as amended, the Education Improvement Act of 1969 (Chapter 6.8 (commencing with Section 6499.200) of this division), the Professional Development and Program Improvement Act of 1968 (Article 3.6 (commencing with Section 13355) of Chapter 2 of Division 10), the Special Teacher Employment Programs (Article 4 (commencing with Section 6481) of Chapter 6.5 of this division), and any other state or federal act which provides funds to assist in the reading program for grades 1, 2, and 3.

5774.2     Application for funds, coordinated project or program for use of funds

Any school district making an application for appointment of a specialist teacher shall use the consolidated application form to make application for funds under any of the acts specified in Section 5774.1 that will be used to assist in the reading program in grades 1, 2, and 3. The application form shall be accompanied by a single coordinated project or program for all the funds for which application is made, as well as the funds of the district devoted to the project or programs.

5774.3     Approval of coordinated project and program

The coordinated project and program shall be approved as required by law and regulations adopted by the State Board of Education.

5774.4     Scope of coordinated project or program

The coordinated project or program shall include a specialist teacher, and other educational component that is approved by the State Board of Education, including, but not limited to, teacher aides, tutors, interns, diagnosticians, nonconsumable and consumable materials and equipment, and administration, supervision or coordination. Each coordinated project or program shall include provisions for evaluation.

5774.7     Insufficient funds for SHARE programs and programs under this chapter, reduction of amounts allocable under this chapter, priorities

If there are not sufficient funds to fully fund the SHARE programs established pursuant to Chapter 1199 of the Statutes of 1970 and programs operated under this chapter as budgeted for the 1971-1972 fiscal year, the Superintendent of Public Instruction shall, insofar as necessary, reduced the amounts allocable under the programs conducted pursuant to this chapter according to the following schedule of priorities:

1. He shall first reduct the amount to be expanded for scholarship grants for teachers under Article 6 (commencing with Section 5794) of this chapter.

2. He shall next reduce the amount to be expended for allotments for professional school librarians under Article 7 (commencing with Section 5798) of this chapter.

3. He shall next reduce the amount to be expended for salary increases under Section 5788.

5775.   Nomination by governing board or petition by certificated employee

The governing board of any school district maintaining grades 1, 2, and 3 in elementary schools may, in writing, nominate to the mission for Teacher Preparation and Licensing qualified certificated employees of the district for the position of specialist teacher. The nominations shall be based upon the observed performance of the teacher in instructing elementary school pupils to read, and the written nominations to the commission shall so attest.

Any certificated employee of a school district who has not been so nominated may, in writing, petition the commission to be appointed a specialist teacher. Thereupon, the commission shall appoint a panel of three persons, selected on the basis of criteria established by rules and regulations of the commission, who shall observe the performance of the employee in the classroom, and either nominate the employee for the position of specialist teacher or deny such nomination.

5776.   Notification of written examination

Each certificated employee nominated for the position of specialist teacher shall be notified of the time and place at which a written examination will be held to determine whether such employee is qualified for appointment as a specialist teacher.

5777.   Selection and administration of written examination

The Commission for Teacher Preparation and Licensing shall designate a written examination to be administered by the Department of Education to each person nominated for the position of specialist teacher. The examination shall be one designed to test the knowledge of the nominee concerning the various approaches and techniques which have been determined by competent authority to be most effective in imparting reading instruction to young school pupils, and concerning the appropriate selection of various techniques to meet the requirements of different pupils. Such an examination shall be administered on a statewide basis at least once in each school year. For such purposes, the commission may select an examination prepared by any competent public or private person, organization, or agency.

5778.    Certificates for passing the examination

Certificated school district employees nominated pursuant to Section 5775, who are determined by the department to have passed the examination prescribed by Section 5777, shall forthwith be granted certificates entitling them to accept employment as specialist teachers in reading.

5778.3    Teacher selection committee, members, expenses, proceedings, qualifications of nominees

As an alternative to the examination and nomination procedure provided for by Sections 5775, 5776, 5777, and 5778, certificated school district employees qualified under this section may be examined for possible selection as specialist teachers in reading by a specialist teacher selection committee. A specialist teacher selection committee may be appointed by the governing board of any school district which maintains elementary schools. It shall be comprised of five members, including one college or university authority in the field of reading instruction, three district or county office personnel knowledgeable in reading instruction and in areas of human relationships, and one district administrator or supervisor. The reasonable and necessary expenses of the members of the committee shall be paid by the school district establishing the committee. The committee shall conduct appropriate proceedings to inquire into the qualifications of nominees qualified for selection as specialist teachers in reading. Each nominee shall, in order to be selected as a specialist teacher in reading meet the following minimum requirements:

(a) Completed two years of successful teaching in the primary grades, kindergarten and grades 1 to 3, inclusive.

(b) Fully credentialed by the State of California to teach in the primary grades, kindergarten and grades 1 to 3, inclusive.

(c) Successfully completed the following college or university courses:

(1) A basic course in the teaching of elementary school reading.
(2) A course in the diagnosis and remediation of reading disabilities.

(3) A course in directed clinical practice in the remediation of reading disabilities.

Such course may be concurrent with the first year as a specialist teacher in reading.

5778.5    Certificates for specialist teachers in reading

Certificated school district employees nominated pursuant to Section 5778.3 shall forthwith be granted certificates entitling them to accept employment as specialist teachers in reading.

5779.    Testing of pupils in grades 1, 2, and 3; national norms; duties of State Board of Education

The State Board of Education shall require each school district to administer uniform tests to each pupil not later than his third month of attendance in the first grade. The first-grade entry level test shall obtain a composite estimate for each pupil of skills related to learning and memory, attention, visual perception, and auditory comprehension. The answer sheets shall be transmitted to the Department of Education for scoring. If no published test is deemed suitable, the State Board of Education may combine parts of available tests or develop a new test.

The State Board of Education shall also require each school district to administer uniform tests in reading annually to pupils in grades 2 and 3. Such tests shall be recommended by the Department of Education and shall be submitted to the State Board of Education for approval and adoption. If no published test is deemed suitable the Department of Education may combine parts of available tests or develop a new test. Any test so adopted shall be equated to nationally normed tests so that the performance of California pupils may be compared to that of a national sample. The tests which have been approved and adopted by the board shall be printed or purchased and distributed to the various school districts in the state by the Department of Education. The answer sheets shall be transmitted to the Department of Education for scoring.

The State Board of Education shall develop a testing method that will obtain an accurate estimate of statewide performance of pupils in grades 2 and 3 in reading. Under such a testing method, the Department of Education shall determine whether pupils in a given school shall be administered the entire test or whether the pupils shall be administered a portion of the test which will be representative of all test objectives, goals, or categories of items on the entire test.

The procedure required by this section shall be implemented not later than the 1975-76 school year.

The State Board of Education shall determine the form in which the answer sheets for the first-grade entry level test shall be transmitted to the Department of Education for scoring, and the form in which the answer sheets for the uniform tests in reading for grades 2 and 3 shall be transmitted to the Department of Education for scoring.

The State Board of Education shall analyze the progress achieved by third grade pupils using the first-grade entry level test results as a basis for identifying comparable pupils receiving various kinds of reading instruction.

The State Board of Education shall adopt rules and regulations governing the time, place, methods for administration of the testing program under this article.

Pupils who have been determined to be mentally retarded, as defined in this code, shall be exempted for the testing requirement imposed by this chapter.

Pupils who have been determined to be educationally handicapped, as defined in this code, shall be subject to the testing requirement imposed by this chapter, except such pupils shall be tested separately from regular pupils. The Department of Education shall annually prepare a comparative analysis of the scores or results of tests administered to educationally handicapped pupils and regular pupils. The Department of Education shall annually report to the Legislature the scores or results of the tests administered to educationally handicapped pupils.

The tests administered pursuant to this article shall be employed to determine each school district's quota of specialist reading teachers, as required by Article 4 (commencing with Section 5781) of this chapter.

Commencing with tests administered in the 1972-1973 school year, school districts shall submit answer sheets and related pupil information on a per-school basis.

5779.2    Use and inclusion of test scores on pupil's cumulative school record

Scores for individual pupils on the first grade entry level test shall not be used by school districts or teachers for individual diagnosis or placement or as a basis for any other decision which would affect the pupil's elementary school experience. Scores from this test shall not in any manner be included on the pupil's cumulative school record.

The State Board of Education shall determine which, if any, of the scores attained by pupils on the tests administered in grades 2 and 3 may be recorded on the pupil's cumulative school record.

5779.3    Pupil performance in reading during grades 1, 2, and 3; methods of assessment; annual report

The State Board of Education shall direct each school district to report annually its methods used to assess pupil performance in reading during grades 1, 2, and 3. The Department of Education shall assist the school districts to improve their local programs of assessing pupil performance in reading.

5780.    Remedial readers' scores, evaluation of reading program, report to Legislature

The scores of tests provided pursuant to Section 5779 of those pupils in grades two and three who have participated in a remedial program shall be maintained and treated separately.

From a study of the results of these tests in districts which conduct a basic reading program pursuant to this chapter, and the test results in districts which do not conduct such a program, the Superintendent of Public Instruction shall evaluate basic reading programs, and he shall report his findings annually to the State Board of Education.

The State Board of Education shall report its findings regarding the implementation of, and experience under, basic reading programs, together with any recommendations for any adjustments in the program, to the Legislature at each regular session. This report and the report required pursuant to Section 12848 may be consolidated into a single annual report.

5780.1    Substitution of grade specification for administration of specific tests, report

Except for the first-grade entry level test required by Section 5779, the State Board of Education may replace the grade specification for the administration of specific tests pursuant to this article with a specification of age or time elapsed since the pupil entered school where such a specification is more consistent with patterns of school organization.

The Department of Education shall submit a report to the Joint Legislative Budget Committee explaining the reasons for replacing the grade specification. The report shall be submitted at least six months prior to any such change.

5781     Quota for each district

Each school district which maintains grades 1, 2, and 3 at the elementary level shall compute a basic quota of certificated employees to be appointed specialist teachers; of one such employee for each 125 units of average daily attendance in grades 1, 2, and 3 and any additional fraction thereof; provided that:

(a) With respect to districts maintaining more than one school, each of which has an average daily attendance in grades 1, 2, and 3 of less than 50, the quota shall be one such employee for each 100 units of the average daily attendance in grades 1, 2, and 3 in those schools.

(b) With respect to all school districts in a county with an average daily attendance in grades 1, 2, and 3 of less than 50, the quota shall be one specialist teacher for each 100 units of average daily attendance in grades 1, 2, and 3 in those districts.

5782     Quota increase for districts with low pupil scores

For the 1967-68 school year and school years thereafter, for any school district in which thirty percent (30%) or more of the first grade pupils received scores falling below the first quartile of scores established on a statewide basis for the tests administered during the preceding school year pursuant to Section 5779, the basic quota established pursuant to Section 5781 shall be increased by one specialist teacher for each 300 units of average daily attendance in grades 1, 2, and 3, and fractional part thereof, maintained by the district.

For the 1967-68 school year and school years thereafter any school district in which forty percent (40%) or more of the first grade pupils received scores falling below the first quartile of scores established on a statewide basis for the tests administered during the preceding school year pursuant to Section 5779, the basic quota established pursuant to Section 5781 shall be increased as ordered by the Department of Education following an investigation of the circumstances of the district.

5783     Maximum limit on quota

Each school district maintaining grades 1, 2, and 3 may employ specialist teachers in number not to exceed one hundred ten percent (110%) of the basic quota established for the district pursuant to Sections 5781 and 5782.

5784     Status and conditions of employment

Persons serving in the employ of school districts as specialist teachers under this chapter shall be considered as classroom teachers for purposes of all laws dealing with permanent status of certificated employees in the employment of school districts.

Such a specialist teacher employed by a school district may elect to serve for a period of not to exceed two consecutive school years in the employ of other school districts as a specialist teacher, in which case the district of the teacher's regular employment shall afford him a leave of absence for such period, and the teacher shall retain in personnel rights accumulated by him in the employ of such district of regular employment. Such employment with another district shall be pursuant to a written contract for a term of one school year, which contract may be renewed for an additional school year.

5785     Specialist teacher employed by a school district with an average daily attendance in grades 1, 2, and 3 of less than 50, shall serve under the direction of the county superintendent of schools.

5786     Qualified teachers under the direction of specialist teachers

The governing board of a school district employing specialist teachers may employ qualified teachers who shall serve under the direction of the specialist teachers in instructing pupils in reading.

5787     Relief from regular duties, specific duties listed

Specialist teachers employed by a school district shall be relieved of all regular teaching and administrative responsibilities and shall devote their full time in performance of the following responsibilities, which shall be directed to training pupils to attain reading ability essential to success in studies to be undertaken beyond the grade 3 level:

(a) Supplementing the reading instruction otherwise provided in regular classes for all pupils in grade 1.

(b) Providing instruction to small groups of pupils, and to individual pupils, in grades 2 and 3 who have been determined to have reading disabilities.

(c) Administering reading tests to be given pupils in grades 2 and 3 under Article 3 (commencing with Section 5779) of this chapter.

5787:5     In-service training, instructional techniques of specialist teachers

School districts shall establish in-service training program to provide an opportunity for elementary school teachers of the district to observe, on a regular basis, the instructional techniques of the specialist teachers.

5788     Increase in annual salary

The annual salary of a specialist teacher, employed as such by a school district for a school year, shall be increased by two hundred fifty dollars ($250) over that otherwise payable to him under his regular contract of employment with the district in which he is regularly employed.

Such sum shall be paid by the school district in a lump sum payment to the specialist reading teacher, no later than June 30 of each fiscal year, and the warrant on which the payment is made shall clearly identify the purpose for which the payment is being made with words to the effect of, "Special Stipend for State Basic Reading Program" appearing on the face of the warrant. Partial lump-sum payments for specialist reading teachers employed for a portion of the school year shall be paid no later than 30 days after the specialist teacher leaves the employ of the district.

5789     Applications by school districts

Beginning with the 1966-67 fiscal year and each fiscal year thereafter, a school district which maintains grades 1, 2, and 3, may apply for an allowance for the employment of specialist teachers. Application shall be made in accordance with rules and regulations adopted by the Superintendent of Public Instruction on forms that he shall furnish.

For programs to be conducted during the 1969-70 fiscal year and each fiscal year therafter, such applications shall be filed with the Superintendent of Public Instruction on or before July 1 in order to be eligible for an allowance during the year.

5790     Approval of application, criteria and minimum standards

Pursuant to its authority under Section 5772, the State Board of Education shall adopt, by rules and regulations, minimum standards of course content for basic reading programs authorized by this chapter, and criteria to be used by the Superintendent of Public Instruction in approving district applications for funds pursuant to Section 5789. No allowance for a special reading program shall be made to a school district unless the Superintendent of Public Instruction approves the district application and certifies that the minimum standards and criteria of the State Board of Education are met by the district.

Beginning with the 1969-70 fiscal year each fiscal year therafter, the Superintendent of Public Instruction shall notify each district of his action on the application, including the estimated allowance to be provided based upon the application filed pursuant to Section 5789. Such notice shall be given to each district prior to September 1 following the receipt of the application. The total of the estimated allowances determined pursuant to this section for all applicant districts shall not exceed the funds appropriated therefor.

The Superintendent shall not disapprove any application on the basis of the methodology of providing basic reading instruction pursuant to this chapter which the school district has selected.

5791     Warrants upon appropriated funds

Allowances under this article shall be made by the Superintendent of Public Instruction from funds appropriated therefore by the Legislature. The allowances shall be made as early as practicable in the fiscal year and, upon order of the Superintendent of Public Instruction, the State Controller shall draw his warrants upon the money appropriated, in favor of the eligible districts in the amounts ordered.

5792    System of priorities among districts

Allowances under this article shall be made by the Superintendent of Public Instruction in accordance with a system of priorities that he shall by rule and regulation adopt, designed to carry out the intent and purpose of the Legislature stated in Section 5771.

The system shall be designed to give priority to districts in the following order:

(a) First, to insure that the districts participating in the program during the preceding school year which continue to be eligible will not be required to reduce programs below the level of the preceding year.

(b) Second, to insure that applications for expansion of programs and applications for new programs in eligible schools be considered on a priority basis in terms of the percentage of pupils in grade 1 who received scores which fell below the first quartile of scores established on a statewide basis for the tests administered during the preceding school year pursuant to Section 5779.

Allowances computed for a district that received only basic aid in the preceding fiscal year shall be reduced by one-half.

The Superintendent of Public Instruction shall make no allowances in any year in excess of the amount appropriated by the Legislature for the purposes of this chapter.


5792:5    Report

The Superintendent of Public Instruction shall by rule and regulation establish a procedure for each district provided an allowance pursuant to this article to report, on or before April 1 of each year, the program actually maintained. If the Superintendent of Public Instruction finds that the school district failed to conduct the program in full or in part as previously approved, the allowances shall be corrected accordingly.


5793    Allowance

The Superintendent of Public Instruction shall allow to each district eligible to receive an amount equal to the total of salaries to be paid specialist teachers employed by the district computed according to

Section 5793.1 and the amounts computed as salary allotments for professional school librarians.

5793:1   Computation of allowance

The allowance for salaries of specialist reading teachers to each district shall be computed by multiplying the number of specialist reading teachers employed by such district by an amount equivalent to the statewide average salary, as determined by the Superintendent of Public Instruction, paid elementary teachers during the preceding fiscal year plus a sum of two hundred fifty dollars ($250) per teacher. The salary allowance so computed shall not be more than the actual salary paid by the district for the services of the specialist reading teacher.

5794   Application for scholarship grants

Any regularly credentialed teacher in grades 1, 2, or 3 may, pursuant to this article apply for a scholarship grant for teachers of reading. Each scholarship grant shall be in the amount of two hundred fifty dollars ($250).

5795   Grants used for teacher training or approved courses

Scholarship grants shall be made by the State Board of Education upon recommendation of the Superintendent of Public Instruction in accordance with rules and regulations adopted by the State Board of Education. The scholarship grants may be used to meet expenses of the grantee attending any regular session or summer session conducted by an institution accredited for teacher training prupuses by the State Board of Education and enrolling for credit in courses designed to improve the teaching or reading that have been approved by the State Board of Education.

5796   Limit on number of grants awarded

The number of scholarship grants awarded by the State Board of Education in the 1966-67 fiscal year shall not exceed the number of specialist teachers in reading for whom allowances were provided during that year to school districts pursuant to Section 5793. In the 1967-68 fiscal year, the number of scholarship grants awarded shall not exceed one-half of the number of specialist teachers in reading for whom allowances were provided during that year. In the 1968-69 fiscal year and each fiscal year thereafter, the number of scholarship grants awarded shall not exceed one-fourth of the number of specialist teachers in reading for whom allowances were provided during each of such respective fiscal years.

5797   Grants paid from appropriations by Legislature

Scholarship grants awarded shall be paid from the amounts appropriated by the Legislature for the purposes of this chapter.

8551   Areas of study

The adopted course of study for grades 1 through 6 shall include instruction, beginning in grade 1 and continuing through grade 6, in the following areas of study:

(a) English, including knowledge of, and appreciation for literature and the language, as well as the skills of speaking, reading, listening, spelling, handwriting, and composition.

8571   Areas of study

The adopted course of study for grades 7 through 12 shall offer courses in the following areas of study:

(a) English, including knowledge of appreciation for literature, language, and composition, and the skills of reading, listening, and speaking.

12821   Legislative intent

It is the intent of the Legislature in enacting this chapter to determine the effectiveness of school districts and schools in assisting pupils to master the fundamental educational skills towards which instruction is directed. The program of statewide testing shall provide the public, the Legislature, and school districts evaluative information regarding the various levels of proficiency achieved by different groups of pupils of varying socioeconomic backgrounds, so that the Legislature and individual school districts may allocate educational resources in a manner to assure the maximum educational opportunity for all pupils. The program of statewide testing shall identify unusual success or failure and the factors which appear to be responsible, so that appropriate action may be taken at the district and state level to obtain the highest quality education for all public school pupils.

12822    Definitions as used in this chapter:

(a) "Achievement test" means any standardized test which measures or attempts to measure the level of performance which a pupil has attained in one or more courses of study. It shall include (1) tests in basic skills courses administered annually and (2) tests in content courses administered from time to time as designated by the State Board of Education.

(b) "Physical performance test" means any test which measures or attempts to measure the physical fitness of a pupil.

(c) "Testing program" means the systematic achievement testing of all pupils in grades 6 and12, and the physical performance testing of all pupils in any three grades designated by the State Board of Education, required by this chapter in all schools within each school district by means of tests designated by the State Board of Education.

(d) "Basic skills courses" means those subjects which involve, among other skills, memorization and mastery of specific functions, including but not limited to, reading, spelling, basic mathematics, and effectiveness of written expression.

(e) "Content courses" means those subjects which require the integration of factual matter, logical analysis, the solution by the student of posed problems, and the communication of ideas, including, but not limited to, literature, history, advanced mathematics, and science.

15:1135    Exemption

Pupils who have been determined to be mentally retarded, or excused from attending regular classes in a public school as prescribed by this title shall be exempt from the testing requirement prescribed . . .

15:1024    Oral and silent reading

As part of its training in developing reading skills, each public school shall devote reasonable amounts of time to oral and silent reading in grades one through eight.

## COLORADO

22:7:101    Short title: This article shall be known and may be cited as the Educational Accountability Act of 1971

22:7:102    Legislative declaration

(1) The general assembly declares that the purpose of this article is to institute an accountability program to define and measure quality in education and thus to help the public schools of Colorado to achieve such quality and to expand the life opportunities and options of the students of this state; further, the purpose is to provide to local school boards assistance in helping their school patrons to determine the relative value of their school program as compared to its cost.

(2) The general assembly further declares that the educational accountability program developed under this article should be designed to measure objectively the adequacy and efficiency of the educational programs offered by the public schools. The program should begin by developing broad goals and specific performance objectives for the educational process and by identifying the activities of schools which can advance students toward these goals and objectives. The program should then develop a means for evaluating the achievements and performance of students. It is the belief of the general assembly that in developing the evaluation mechanism, the following approaches, as a minimum, should be explored:

(a) Means for determining whether decisions affecting the education process are advancing or impeding student achievement;

(b) Appropriate testing procedures to provide relevant comparative data at least in the fields of reading. language skills, and mathematical skills;

(c) The role of the department of education in assisting school districts to strengthen their educational programs;

(d) Reporting to students, parents, boards of education, educators, and the general public on the educational performance of the public schools and providing data for the appraisal of such performance; and

(e) Provision of information which could help school districts to increase their efficiency in using available financial resources.

## CONNECTICUT

10:15    Maintenance of schools by towns, prescribed courses of study

Public schools shall be maintained in each town for at least one hundred eighty days of actual school sessions during each year. The state board of education may authorize the shortening of any school year on account of an unavoidable emergency. The public schools shall be open to all children over six years of age without discrimination on account of race or color; provided town boards of education may, by vote at a meeting duly called, admit any school children over five years of age or may exclude children who will not attain the age of six years until after the first day of January of any school year. In said schools shall be taught, by teachers legally qualified, reading; spelling; writing; English grammar; geography; arithmetic; United States, state and local history; the duties of citizenship, which shall include a study of the town, state and federal governments; hygiene, including the effects of alcohol and narcotics on health and character; physical and health education, including methods, as presented by the state board of education, to be employed in preventing and correcting bodily deficiency; instruction in the humane treatment and protection of animals and birds and their economic importance, such instruction, when practicable, to be correlated with work in reading, language and nature study; and such other subjects as may be prescribed by the board of education. Courses in health instruction and physical education shall be prepared by the secretary of the state board of education and, when approved by the state board of education, shall constitute the prescribed courses (1949 Rev., 1349).

163.a:    [10.14e (P.A. 76-405, Section 1)] Proficiency examination, enrolled students, examination, reexamination

(a) After September 1, 1977, each student enrolled in the tenth grade in any public high school or in any endowed or incorporated high school or academy, approved pursuant to section 10-34, shall take the proficiency examination given pursuant to section 10-14g.

(b) After September 1, 1979, any student enrolled in the twelfth grade in any such school or academy who has unsuccessfully taken the examination required in subsection (a) of this section shall be reexamined once prior to receiving his high school diploma.

(c) After September 1, 1979, any student enrolled in the twelfth grade in any such school or academy who has not taken the proficiency examination given pursuant to section 10-14g may take such examination.

163.a:     [10-14f (P.A. 76-405, Section 2)] Proficiency examination, unenrolled students, fee, notice

Any person sixteen years of age or older, who is not enrolled (1) in a public high school or an endowed or incorporated high school or academy, approved pursuant to section 10-34, or (2) in an adult education elementary and secondary completion program, may, after September 1, 1978, take the proficiency examination given pursuant to section 10-14g upon application and payment of a non-returnable fee of ten dollars to the state board of education. Any such person who successfully takes such examination shall receive notice from the state board of education certifying that he has successfully taken such examination.

163.a:     [10-14g (P.A. 76-405, Section 3)] Proficiency examination, establishment of means, procedures to administer, offering limitation, regulations

Prior to September 1, 1977, the state board of education shall, in consultation with any interested parties, (1) establish a means to examine proficiency of performance in basic verbal and quantitative skills, and (2) develop procedures to administer, grade and report the results of examinations to be offered for the purpose of testing such skills and to be taken pursuant to sections 10-14e or 10-14f. Such examinations shall be graded either "Pass" or "Fail". Such examinations shall be offered not more than four times in any calendar year, provided the same examination shall be offered to all students and other persons taking it on the same date. Said board shall promulgate such regulations as are necessary to carry out the purposes of sections 10-14e to 10-14h.

163.a     [10-14h (P.A. 76-405, Section 4)] Proficiency examination, effective date

Sections 10-14e to 10-14h shall take effect upon receipt by the state board of education of not less than fifty thousand dollars in federal or private funding for the purposes of this act, provided if such funding is not granted on or before January 1, 1977, this act shall not become effective.

## DELAWARE

14:3101   Definition: (7) "Learning disability" means a disorder in 1 or more of the basic psychological or physiological processes involved in understanding and in using spoken or written languages. These may be manifested in disorders of listening, thinking, talking, reading, writing, spelling or arithmetic. They include, but are not limited to, conditions which have been referred to as perceptual handicaps, brain injury, minimal brain dysfunction, dyslexia and/or developmental aphasia. They do not include learning problems which are due primarily to visual, hearing or orthopedic handicaps, to emotional disturbance if these are provided for elsewhere or to mental retardation or to environmental disadvantage.

## FLORIDA

229.814   Secondary Level Examination Program

(1) The State Board of Education shall adopt rules which prescribe performance standards and provide for comprehensive examinations to be administered to candidates for high school equivalency diplomas and for individual examinations in the subject areas required for high school graduation. These rules shall include, but not be limited to, provisions for fees, frequency of examinations, and procedures for retaking an examination upon unsatisfactory performance.

(2) The Department of Education is authorized to award high school equivalency diplomas to candidates who meet the performance standards prescribed by the state board.

(3) Each district school board shall offer and administer the high school equivalency diploma examinations and the subject area examinations to all candidates pursuant to rules of the state board.

(4) Any candidate who is awarded an equivalency diploma shall be exempted from the compulsory school attendance requirements of Section 232.01.

(5) Each district school board shall develop in cooperation with the area community college board of trustees, a plan for the provision of advance instruction for those students who attain satisfactory performance on the high school equivalency examination or the subject area examinations or who demonstrate through other means a

readiness to engage in postsecondary level academic work. The plan shall include provisions for the equitable distribution of generated funds to cover personnel, maintenance and other costs of offering the advanced instruction. Priority shall be given to programs of advanced instruction offered in high school facilities. (Laws 1975, c. 75-130, Section 1, effective July 1, 1975. Amended by Laws 1976, c. 76-223, Section 9, effective July 1, 1976.)

232.245  Pupil progression

(1) By July 1, 1977, each district school board shall establish a comprehensive program for pupil progression which shall be based upon an evaluation of each pupil's performance standards approved by the state board.

(2) The district program for pupil progression shall be based upon local goals and objectives which are compatible with the state's plan for education and which supplement the minimum performance standards approved by the State Board of Education. Particular emphasis, however, shall be placed upon the pupil's mastery of the basic skills, especially reading, before he is promoted from the 3rd, 5th, 8th and 11th grades. Other pertinent factors considered by the teacher before recommending that a pupil progress from one grade to another shall be prescribed by the district school board in its rules.

(3) Beginning with the 1978-79 school year, each district school board shall establish standards for graduation from its secondary schools. Such standards shall include, but not be limited to, mastery of the basic skills and satisfactory in functional literacy as determined by the State Board of Education and the completion of the minimum number of credits required by the district school board. Each district shall develop procedures for the remediation of (the deficiencies of)[1] those students who are unable to meet such standards. Based on these standards, each district shall provide for the awarding of certificates of attendance and may provide for differentiated diplomas to correspond with the varying achievement levels or competencies of its secondary students. (Added by Laws 1976, c. 76-223, Section 15, effective July 1, 1976.)

233:055  Remedial reading education plan

(1) Short title: This section shall be known and may be cited as The Florida Remedial Reading Education Act of 1971.

(2) Commissioner's planning budget: The commissioner of education

shall develop and transmit at least 30 days prior to the 1972 regular session of the legislature, to members of the state board of education, the president of the senate, the speaker of the house of representatives, and the chairman of the senate and house committees on education a detailed plan for implementing a remedial reading program. The plan shall include provisions for maximum participation by the school districts and the Department of Health and Rehabilitative Services in the development of remedial reading programs. The plan shall be in detail for the 1972-73 fiscal year, and the funds for projects for 1972-1973 shall be included in the legislative budget of the state board submitted to the Governor as chief budget officer of the state for the 1972-1973 fiscal year.

(3) Remedial reading program

(a) In the event that funds for projects are included in the 1972-1973 budgets, the state board of education shall adopt policies and regulations by which each school board and the department of health and rehabilitative services may apply to the department of education funds to be used in a remedial reading program. The application shall contain a comprehensive plan for the use of such funds, which shall:

1. Include pre-testing and post-testing of reading level and ability;
2. Describe what programs, teaching methods, or techniques will be used, such as programmed tutoring, individualized instruction, or any other method of demonstrated success;
3. Provide for control groups at each level to enable a measurement of the effectiveness of the remedial programs; and
4. Demonstrate that the school board has fully utilized all other sources of revenue and the assistance of all volunteer aid offered by individuals and public and private organizations and has effectively coordinated same.

(b) Priority funding will be given to those programs which:

1. Offer the greatest likelihood of remedying the difference between current reading level and chronological age average attainment;
2. Serve the largest number of pupils; and
3. Utilize to the maximum other sources of funds.

(4) Technical assistance provided

Upon the request of any school board, the department shall provide such technical assistance to the school board as is necessary to develop and submit a plan for a remedial reading program. The department may use its own staff or such consultants as may be necessary to accomplish this purpose.

(5) Commissioner's report

The commissioner of education shall transmit to members of the state board of education, the president of the senate, the speaker of the house of representatives, and the chairmen of the house and senate committees on public school education an appraisal of the funded programs as to effectiveness, efficiency, and utilization of resources. This appraisal shall include an evaluation of current reading ability in the public schools and the change made in status during the past year (1971, c. 71-273, 1-5, effective July 1, 1971.)

233:056     Instructional programs for visually handicapped students

(1) The division of elementary and secondary education of the department of education is authorized to establish a coordinating unit and instructional materials center for visually handicapped children and youth to provide staff and resources for the coordination, cataloging, standardizing, producing, procuring, storing, and distributing of braille, large print, tangible apparatus, and other specialized educational materials needed by blind and partially sighted students. The coordinating unit shall have as its major purpose the improvement of instructional programs for visually handicapped students.

(2) The unit shall be operated either directly by the division of elementary and secondary education or through a contractual agreement with a local education agency, under regulations and procedures adopted by the state board of education.

233:057     Developmental reading and language arts program

(1) Legistlative intent: The legislature recognizes that reading is one of the communication skills which facilitiates learning in all areas of the curriculum. It further recognizes the need for coordination of developmental reading programs in public schools. In order to make this possible, the legislature intends to provide for the employment and training of reading and language arts resource specialists. Funds shall be allocated to the department of education to be distributed to local school districts for elementary school programs with emphasis being placed on prevention of reading and language arts difficulties.

(2) Certification: The state board of education shall adopt regulations granting certification to those who qualify as reading and language arts resource specialists. Certification shall be granted to those who have had a minimum of three (3) years' teaching experience and who:

(a) In the judgement of the state board of education possess the qualifications and necessary experience to serve in the position; or

(b) Have successfully completed programs approved by the department of education.

(3) Duties and responsibilities: The duties and responsibilities of reading and language arts resource specialists shall include, but not be limited to, the following:

(a) Assist the principal and classroom teachers in organizing and managing reading as part of the many content areas of the curriculum.

(b) Assist in preparing a school's developmental reading and language arts program.

(c) Provide for in-service staff development.

(4) Training: Pursuant to policies and regulation to be adopted by the state board of education:

(a) Colleges of education: Colleges of education shall develop programs leading to certification of teachers to serve as reading and language arts resource specialists.

(b) Local school districts

1. Each local school district or a combination of districts may submit to the commissioner a proposed program designed to train and employ reading and language arts resource specialists, including therewith a statement of the number of individuals to be included in the program, an itemized statement of the estimated total cost of the program, and a copy of a school board resolution indicating its intention to provide at least one half of the total cost of the program if approved by the commissioner.

2. Upon the request of any local school district, the department shall provide such technical assistance to the school district as is necessary to develop and submit a proposed program for identification and training of reading and language arts resource specialists. The department may use its own staff or such consultants as may be necessary to accomplish this purpose.

3. The commissioner shall review and approve, disapprove, or resubmit to the local school district for modification all proposed programs submitted. For those programs approved, the commissioner shall authorize distribution of funds in an amount not to exceed one half of the total cost of the proposed program.

4. The commissioner shall, at least thirty (30) days prior to each regular session of the legislature, transmit to members of

the state board of education, the president of the senate, the
speaker of the house of representatives, and the chairmen of
the senate and house committees on public school education
an appraisal of the funded programs as to effectiveness, efficiency, and utilization of resources, including therewith a
statement of the overall program for the coming fiscal year,
the recommended level of funding for the program for that
year, and any other recommendations deemed by the commissioner to be appropriate.

## GEORGIA

### 32:606a    Compensatory education

(a) The State Board of Education shall promulgate rules, regulations
and standards and establish the terms and conditions necessary to
implement programs of compensatory education. Compensatory
education shall include, but shall not be limited to, programs of
remedial reading, mathematics, and such other programs as are needed.

(b) The State Board of Education shall annually determine the number
of students needing compensatory education and the estimated State
cost of such program for the next fiscal year, and submit such information to the Office of Planning and Budget.

### 32:608a    Adult education

(a) The State Board of Education shall maintain an adult general
education program within the State. This program shall provide
instruction in basic skills and subjects to individuals 18 years of age
and older who have left school and who have less than an eighth
grade education or its equivalent. Instruction in a variety of skills
and subjects may be provided for individuals who have more than an
eighth grade education or its equivalent. Priority shall be given to
elimination of illiteracy in the State and to the attainment of a
General Educational Development (GED) equivalency diploma. Programs of general education for adults should serve to improve the
ability of the individual to profit from occupational training and
meet adult responsibilities more effectively.

### 32:2401    Duties, reports, authority to use funds, etc.

It shall be the duty of the State Board of Education and it shall have the power to make researches, collect data and statistics, and procure surveys of any and all communities, districts, or vicinities of the State, looking to the obtaining of a more detailed, definite and particular knowledge as to the true conditions of the State with regard to its adult illiteracy, and to encourage and promote the establishment of schools for adult illiterates and to cooperate with other State, county or Federal agencies in the elimination of adult illiteracy; and report regularly the results of its labors to the General Assembly; and to interest persons and institutions in the dispensation of any and all funds and endowments of whatsoever kind which will or may aid in the elimination of the adult illiteracy of the State, and do or perform any other act which in their discretion will contribute to the elimination of the State's adult illiteracy by means of education, instruction and enlightenment; and said board shall be empowered to receive, accept, hold, own, distribute and expend, to the end of educating, instructing, enlightening and assisting in the education, instruction and enlightenment of illiterate persons in the State of Georgia, any and all funds or other things of value with which it may be endowed or may otherwise receive; and in the expenditure and disbursement thereof said board shall be controlled by such expedient and discreet regulations as it may from time to time adopt: Provided, however, that any and all such funds which may come to the hands of said board shall be expended in keeping with the general purposes of this Chapter.

## 32:2501    Schools authorized

The county commissioners, or the judges of the probate courts of such counties as have no commissioners, shall have authority in their discretion to provide for the carrying on in their respective counties of schools for instructing adult illiterates in the elementary branches of an English education only.

## HAWAII

## 301:2    Scope of adult education courses offered

As rapidly as facilities are available and interest is developed, courses shall be initiated in the following fields:

(1) Basic elementary education: A foundation program in reading

and speaking English, writing, and arithmetic for persons with no schooling or only primary grade training

## IDAHO

**33:1607    Americanization of adults**

The board of trustees of any school district is authorized to provide instruction for Americanization of adult residents of the state, including classes in reading, writing, and speaking the English language; the principles of the Constitution of the United States, American history, and such other subjects as deemed desirable for making, of such adults, better American citizens. The expense of such instruction shall be a lawful charge against the maintenance and operation funds of the district.

## ILLINOIS

**14-1.03A    Definition: Handicapped Children, children with specific learning disabilities**

"Children with Specific Learning Disabilities" means children between the ages of 3 and 21 years who have a disorder in one or more of the basic psychological processes involved in understanding or in using language, spoken or written, which disorder may manifest itself in imperfect ability to listen, think, speak, read, write, spell or do mathematical calculations. Such disorders include such conditions as perceptual handicaps, brain injury, minimal brain dysfunction, dyslexia, and developmental asphasia. Such term does not include children who have learning problems which are primarily the result of visual, hearing or motor handicaps, or mental retardation, emotional disturbance or environmental disadvantage.

## INDIANA

No code provision found.

## IOWA

**257:25    Educational standards**

In addition to the responsibiliities of the state board of public instruction and the state superintendent of public instruction under other provisions of the Code, the state board of public instruction shall, except as otherwise provided in this section, establish standards, regulations, and rules for the approval of all public, parochial, and private nursery, kindergarten, elementary, junior high, and high schools and all area vocational schools, area community colleges, and public community or junior colleges in Iowa. With respect to area or public community or junior colleges, such standards, regulations, and rules shall be established by the state board of public instruction and the state board of regents, acting jointly. Such approval standards, regulations, and rules shall prescribe and implement the minimum curriculum described below.

1. Nursery school activities shall be designed to help children use and manage their bodies, extend their interests and understanding of the world about them, work and play with others and to express themselves.

2. Kindergarten programs shall include experiences designed to develop emotional and social living, protection and development of physical being, growth in expression, and language arts and communication readiness.

3. The following areas shall be taught in the elementary school, grades one through six: Language arts, including reading, handwriting, spelling, oral and written English, and literature; social studies, including geography, history of the United States and Iowa, cultures of other peoples and nations, and American citizenship, including the elementary study of national, state, and local government in the United States; mathematics; science, including conservation of natural resources; health and physical education, including the effects of alcohol, narcotics, and poisons on the human body; music; art.

4. The following shall be taught in grades seven and eight as a minimum program: Science; mathematics; social studies; language arts which may include spelling, grammar oral and written composition, and other communication subjects; reading; physical education; music; art.

5. Provision for special education services and programs, which may be shared by public schools, shall be made for children requiring special education, who are or would otherwise be enrolled in kindergarten through grade eight of such schools.

6. School districts with organized and administered junior high schools not limited to grades seven and eight must include the aforementioned minimum program for grades seven and eight regardless of the organizational structure of the district.

7. A high school minimum program, grades nine through twelve, shall teach annually the following as a minimum program:

280:3    Common school studies

Reading, writing, spelling, arithmetic, grammar, geography, physiology, United States history, history of Iowa, and the principles of American government shall be taught in all such schools.

259A.1    Tests: The department of public instruction shall cause to be made available for qualified individuals a high school equivalency diploma. The diploma shall be issued on the basis of satisfactory competence as shown by tests covering: The correctness and effectiveness of expression; the interpretation of reading material in the social studies; interpretation of reading materials in the natural sciences; interpretation of literary materials; and general mathematical ability.

## KANSAS

No code provisions found.

## KENTUCKY

157:200:    Definition: special educational programs

(e) "Children with learning disabilities" are those children who have a disorder in one or more of the basic psychological processes involved in understanding or using language, spoken or written, which disorder may manifest itself in imperfect ability to listen, think, speak, read, write, spell, or do mathematical calculations. Such disorders include such conditions as perceptual handicaps, brain injury, minimal brain dysfunction, dyslexia, and developmental aphasia. Such term does not include children who have learning problems which are primarily the result of visual, hearing or motor handicaps, of mental retardation, of emotional disturbance, or of environmental disadvantage.

## LOUISIANA

### 17:153-154.    Curriculum, length of school periods

The branches of spelling, reading, writing, drawing, arithmetic, geography, grammar, United States history, and health, including the evil effects of alcohol and narcotics, shall be taught in every elementary school. In addition to these, such other branches shall be taught as the state board of education, or the provisions of the state constitution, may require. The minimum daily session, exclusive of all recesses, of every public school shall be five hours, provided that this shall not be construed so as to prevent half-day sessions where the school accommodations are insufficient for all the pupils of the district in a whole-day session. Nor shall it interfere with any arrangement made for the conduct of kindergarten schools; provided that in the parish of Orleans the school board may fix the hours of the daily session of the public schools. A school week shall consist of five days and a school month of twenty days.

### 391.1    Statement of purpose

It is the intent and purpose of the legislature to provide for the development and implementation of educational evaluation and assessment procedures for the public schools of the state of Louisiana. To accomplish this purpose it is the intent of the legislature:

(1) To provide for the establishment of procedures for shared educational accountability in the public educational system of Louisiana.

(2) To assure that education programs operated in the public schools of Louisana lead to the attainment of established objectives for education.

(3) To provide for a uniform system of evaluation of the performance of school personnel.

(4) To provide information for accurate analysis of the cost associated with public education programs.

(5) To provide information for an analysis of the differential effectiveness of instructional programs.

391.2    Definitions

As used in this Part, the following words, terms, and phrases shall have the meaning ascribed to them in this Section, except when the context clearly indicates a different meaning:

(1) "Communication skills" means the arts of reading, writing, and speaking the English language.

(2) "Basic computational skills" means skill in basic arithmetic and mathematics.

(3) "School board" means a parish or city school board.

(4) "Public education" means the public elementary and secondary level educational programs funded by the state and local government in the public schools and other institutions providing educational programs.

(5) "Public schools" means the public elementary and secondary schools governed by the parish and city schools boards and under the supervision of the State Board of Elementary and Secondary Education.

(6) "School district" means the area of each parish or municipality under the jurisdiction of a school board.

(7) "School personnel" means the teachers, librarians, counselors, administrators, and other professional personnel of the public schools of the state including members of the professional staff of the State Department of Education.

(8) "Educational accountability" means the respective responsibilities and duties of local school boards, their members, adminstrators, principals, teachers and other personnel; the State Board of Elementary and Secondary Education; the Department of Education and its personnel; parents, students and any other governing authority and as otherwise provided by the constitution and laws of this state. Educational accountability shall be shared as provided by R.S. 17:391.3 and otherwise provided therein.

391.3    Program for educational accountability

A. The superintendent of education shall develop a program for educational accountability for the public schools of the state no later than January 1, 1977.

The program shall be approved by the State Board of Elementary and Secondary Education no later than January 15, 1977, and each year thereafter. The approved program shall be submitted annually to the Joint Legislative Committee on Education of the Louisiana Legislature for review.

B. Specifically, but without limitation, the program shall:

(1) Establish and provide for implementation of a procedure for the continuous identification, examination, and improvement of the goals of education in the state.

(2) Establish basic uniform statewide educational objectives for each grade level and subject area, including but not limited to, reading, writing, and mathematics.

(3) Identify performance objectives which will lead directly to the achievement of the stated goals.

(4) Develop evaluation instruments, including, but not limited to, tests to provide the evaluation required.

(5) Develop and implement an overall evaluation design to provide for continuous and comprehensive review of the progress of school pupils toward the established goals and objectives, the evaluation to be conducted by teaching staff members of the school district under the direction of the chief school administrator of the district.

(6) Provide for an annual report by the chief school administrator of each school district to the State Board of Elementary and Secondary Education of the results of the evaluation of the progress of pupils accomplished as provided in Paragraph (4) above.

(7) In order to provide for the orderly implementation of the accountability program, identification and establishment of statewide educational objectives for each grade level and subject area, and evaluation of the achievement of these objectives shall be accomplished for the school year 1977-1978, for the subject area of reading; for the school year 1978-1979, for the additional subject area of writing; and for the school year 1979-1980, for the additional subject area of mathematics; and thereafter other subject areas shall be added.

C. Pursuant to this Section, the Department of Education and local school boards and administrators shall develop goals and objectives for the school districts in conjunction with those of the accountability plan.

D. The State Board of Elementary and Secondary Education shall prescribe a system for reporting to the parents the progress of each pupil, including but not limited to parent-teachers' conferences, report cards, and pupil progress charts.

E. In carrying out the accountability program, the local school boards and the Department of Education shall develop and implement procedures to assist teachers and school personnel and administrators in identifying the status of the physical, intellectual, social and emotional development of each pupil and his needs relative to the areas as well as the special aptitudes and abilities of pupils and of problems which may affect learning. These procedures shall include, but not be limited to teachers' observations; teacher training and consultation; parent-teachers' conferences; union of cumulative pupil records; review of test results, including, but not limited to, those administered pursuant to this Part.

391.4    Pupil proficiency

A. The State Board of Elementary and Secondary Education shall, by January 1, 1977, establish reasonable minimum levels of pupil proficiency in the basic communication and computational skills which shall be integrated into instructional programs. The superintendent of education shall, by January 1, 1978, develop and administer a uniform system of assessment based in part on criterion referenced tests to determine pupil status, pupil progress, and the degree to which such minimum proficiency standards have been met. The local school governing bodies shall cooperate with the superintendent and the Department of Education in the administration of this Section.

B. The school board of each district shall for the 1977-1978 school year and annually thereafter make a public report of the aforementioned assessment results which shall include pupil assessment by grade and subject area for each school in the district. A copy of the district's public report shall be filed with the superintendent of education.

C. The state superintendent of education shall make an annual report of the aforementioned assessment results. Such report shall include, but not be limited to, a report of the assessment results by grade and subject area for each school district of the state, with an analysis and recommendations concerning the costs and differential effectiveness of instructional programs.

D. In addition, the Department of Education shall prepare and submit an annual report to the legislature, containing an analysis, on a district-by-district basis, of the results and test scores of the testing program in the basic skills courses. The report shall include, but shall not be limited to, an analysis of the following operational factors having a substantive relationship to or bearing on such results:

(1) Average class size in grades one to three, inclusive.

(2) Pupil-teacher ratio in grades one to eight, inclusive.

(3) Average scholastic ability as determined by such standards as shall be established by the State Board of Elementary and Secondary Education.

(4) Average transitory factors as derived from dividing the average daily attendance of the district or selected schools by the total annual enrollment of the district.

(5) Analysis of compensatory educational needs in each parish and city school system.

391.5    School personnel assessment and evaluation

A. The department of education, with the approval of the State Board of Elementary and Secondary Education shall develop a set of guidelines for assessment and evaluation of the performance of certified teachers, administrators, and other professional school personnel in the state for adoption by each school board. The State Board of Elementary and Secondary Education, with the assistance of a representative committee of teachers and administrators, shall develop a set of guidelines for assessment and evaluation of the performance of professional personnel in the State Department of Education. The guidelines shall be reviewed by the Joint Legislative Committee on Education of the Louisiana Legislature. Such guidelines shall be submitted by the State Board of Elementary and Secondary Education to the local school boards no later than June 1, 1977, and shall include but not be limited to the following guidelines:

(1) The establishment of criteria of expected teaching performance in each area of teaching and of techniques for the assessment and evaluation of that performance.

(2) Assessment and evaluation of competence of certified teachers as it relates to the established criteria.

(3) A listing of other nonteaching duties normally required to be performed by certified employees as an adjunct to their regular assignments.

(4) The establishment of criteria and the assessment of the performance of other school personnel.

In the development of these guidelines and procedures, the Department of Education shall avail itself of the advice of the state certified teachers and such other school personnel as may be necessary.

B. No later than August 15, 1977, each school board shall adopt a system of personnel evaluation and assessment based on the guidelines submitted by the State Board of Elementary and Secondary Education. Evaluation and assessment of the performance of each certified employee shall be made on a continuing basis, at least once each school year for probationary personnel, and at least every other year for personnel with permanent status. The evaluation shall consist of an appraisement of the performance of the employee in the extension of teaching duties and responsibilities. In the event an employee is considered not performing his duties in a satisfactory manner then the employing authority shall notify the employee in writing of such determination and describe such performance. The employing authority shall thereafter confer with the employee making specific recommendations as to areas of considered unsatisfactory performance of the employee and to assist him to correct such considered deficiencies. Assistance shall include but not be limited to inservice training programs or such other appropriate programs.

C. No evaluation and assessment shall be made except in writing and a copy thereof shall be transmitted to the school employee not later than fifteen days after the evaluation takes place. The employee shall have the right to initiate a written reaction or response to the evaluation. Such response and evaluation shall become a permanent attachment to the single official personnel file for the employee. After the evaluation has been transmitted to the employee and before the end of the school year, a meeting shall be held between the certified employee and the appropriate official of the local governing board in order that the employee may respond to the evaluation and have the opportunity to amend, remove, or strike any inaccurate or invalid information as may be found within the written evaluation and from the employee's personnel file.

D. Copies of the assessment and evaluation report of any school employee retained by the school board are confidential, do not constitute a public record, and shall not be released or shown to any person except:

(1) To said school employee.

(2) To authorized school district officers and employees for all personnel matters and for any hearing which relates to personnel matters.

(3) For introduction in evidence or discovery in any court action between the board and the certified teacher in which either:

(a) The competency of the teacher is at issue.
(b) The assessment and evaluation was an exhibit at a hearing, the result of which is challenged.

The State Board of Elementary and Secondary Education shall make available to the news media and other agencies such data as may be useful for conducting statistical analyses and evaluations of educational personnel, but shall not reveal information pertaining to the assessment and evaluation report of a particular teacher.

E. Each school board shall annually file a report with the State Board of Elementary and Secondary Education containing such information relative to the evaluation of school personnel according to the board guidelines as the board shall direct. Based on such report, the Department of Education shall annually compile a report listing the results of assessments in the various school districts and proposals for the improvement of school personnel and shall file such report with the State Board of Elementary and Secondary Education and with the education committees of the two houses of the legislature.

391.6     Course evaluation

A. From time to time, as the State Board of Elementary and Secondary Education may determine, the Department of Education shall conduct studies of the effectiveness of various courses, in addition to the basic communication and computation skills courses, offered by the public schools of this state. Such studies shall include details of the specific objectives of the courses and the level of achievement attained by students enrolled in such courses and, for this purpose, the board may use the results of any test administered under the provisions of this Part.

B. Upon the completion of such a study by the department of education pursuant to this Section, the department shall report its findings, and recommendations, if any, to the State Board of Elementary and Secondary Education and the legislature not later than January 1 of the year succeeding completion of the study.

C. The department shall maintain the anonymity of all students involved and local school board personnel. The department may make analyses involving other factors, including but not limited to general categories of pedagogies in use, type of district organization, geographic area, socioeconomic data, size of school district, or other analytical items which may prove useful.

D. The governing board of any school district shall cooperate fully with the State Board of Elementary and Secondary Education in making its schools available for such studies; provided, that the

Department of Education shall provide all necessary materials. Such evaluation materials may include texts, books, references, tests, library print and nonprint materials, equipment, and materials. (Added by Acts 1976, No. 709, Section 1.)

391.7    Testing

A. Each school board shall report to the department of education, pursuant to rules and regulations established by this Part and by the State Board of Elementary and Secondary Education pursuant to this Part, the results of all achievement and scholastic aptitude tests administered pursuant to this Part or any other standardized tests administered pursuant to this Part.

B. The districtwide results of such tests, but not the score or relative position of individual pupils, shall be reported by the school board at least once a year at a regularly scheduled meeting.

C. At the request of the State Board of Elementary and Secondary Education, and in accordance with the rules and regulations which the board may adopt, each parish superintendent of schools shall cooperate with and give assistance to individual local schools under his jurisdiction in carrying out the testing programs of such districts and other duties imposed on school boards and school districts by this Part.

D. No city or parish superintendent of schools, nor any principal or teacher of any elementary or secondary school under his charge shall carry on any program of specific preparation of the pupils within the district for the testing program as such or the particular test used therein. The tests shall reflect the objectives and goals adopted for each subject and/or grade level.

E. No provision of this Part shall be construed to mean, or represented to require, that graduation from a high school or promotion to another grade level is in any way dependent upon successful performance on any test administered as a part of the testing program. However, the State Board of Elementary and Secondary Education retains the authority to adopt such requirements.

F. Prior to administration, descriptions of tests and other evaluation instruments, either prescribed by or developed pursuant to this Part, shall be submitted to all school personnel and the parents of all pupils subject to such tests.

108      *Appendix*

391.8     Reports

The State Board of Elementary and Secondary Education shall make
such reports to the legislature in addition to those specifically required
in this Part as it shall deem appropriate and shall be required to make
such recommendations to the legislature as it deems appropriate
concerning appropriate or necessary legislation with respect to the
results of the accountability and assessment programs established by
and pursuant to this Part.

391.9     Public school acreditation

Not later than the 1978-1979 School Year, the superintendent of
education, with the approval of the State Board of Elementary and
Secondary Education, shall develop and institute accreditation standards for public schools based upon the attainment of educational
objectives and goals established by this part; provided, however, that
such accreditation standards shall take into account the educational
advantages and disadvantages imposed by the home and out-of-school
environment upon pupils. The board shall implement a system of
public school accreditation in such school year based on such standards. (By Acts 1976, No. 709, Section 1.)

391.10    Plan adoption, independent reports

All plans and standards adopted pursuant to this Part which involve
adoption by the State Department of Education or by the State
Board of Elementary and Secondary Education of means of measurement and evaluation shall be submitted to no fewer than three
independent authorities in the field.

391.11    Parish pilot programs and participation

The public school accountability and assessment program described
herein shall not become operative in any parish which is presently
implementing a parish pilot educational accountability program until
the expiration of such parish program. However, the parishes of
Acadia, Allen, Beauregrad, Cameron, Calcasieu, Evangeline, Lafayette,
Lafourche, St. Landry, Terrebonne, Vermilion and Jeff Davis may,
in their discretion, either establish or maintain an existing Public
School Accountability and Assessment Program in their respective
parishes or may participate in the statewide Public School Accountability and Assessment Program described in this Part (By Acts 1976.
No. 709, Section 2.)

391.12     Parish exemptions, majority vote

The provisions of this Part shall not apply to the parishes hereinafter listed except with a majority vote of the governing body of the school systems: Iberville, East Baton Rouge, West Baton Rouge, Pointe Coupee, West Feliciana, East Feliciana, Ouachita, Lincoln, Union Jackson, Bienville, Red River, Winn, Grant, St. Helena, Tangipahoa, Wards 7, 10, and 11 of Rapides, Washington. St. Tammany, Natchitoches, St. Bernard, Plaquemines, Bossier, Webster, Claiborne, Ascension, Livingston, St. James, Jefferson, DeSoto, St. John the Baptist, St. Charles and Lafourche (By Acts 1976, No. 709, Section 5.)

## MAINE

No code provisions found.

## MARYLAND

28A     Program of educational accountability for operation and management of public schools to be established.

(a) Education accountability program: The State Board of Education and State Superintendent of Schools, each board of education and every school system, and every school, shall implement a program of education accountability for the operation and management of the public schools, which shall include the following:

(1) The State Board of Education and the State Superintendent of Schools shall assist each local school board and school system in developing and implementing educational goals and objectives in conformity with statewide educational objectives for subject areas including, but not limited to, reading, writing, and mathematics.

(2) Each school, with the assistance of its local board of education and school system, shall survey the current status of student achievement in reading, language, mathematics, and other areas in order to assess its needs.

(3) Each school shall establish as the basis of its assessment project goals and objectives which are in keeping with the goals and objectives established by its board of education and the State Board of Education.

(4) Each school, with the assistance of its local board of education, the State Board of Education and the State Superintendent of Schools, shall develop programs for meeting its needs on the basis of priorities which it shall set.

(5) Evaluation programs shall concurrently be developed to determine if the goals and objectives are being met.

(6) Reevaluation of programs, goals and objectives shall be regularly undertaken.

(b) Assistance from State Department of Education: The State Department of Education shall assist the local boards of education in establishing this program by providing guidelines for development and implementation of the program by the local boards, and by providing assistance and coordination where needed and requested by those boards.

(c) Beginning on July 1, 1973, the State Board of Education, upon recommendation of the State Superintendent of Schools, shall include in its annual budget request such funds as it deems necessary to carry out the provisions of this section.

(d) During January, 1975, and each January thereafter, the State Superintendent of Schools shall transmit to the Governor and to the General Assembly a report which includes, but is not limited to documentation indicating the progress of the State Department of Education, the local boards of education and each school in the State, toward the achievement of their respective goals and objectives and recommendations for legislation which the State Board of Education and the State Superintendent of Schools deem necessary for the improvement of the quality of education in Maryland (1972, Chapter 359).

98D    Minimum reading levels prescribed

(a) The State Board of Education shall prescribe for each grade two through twelve a minimum level of reading ability which shall progressively rise with each succeeding grade. If a local school board, based upon local assessment of student progress and in conjunction with the Maryland accountability assessment program, determines that a student, in grades three, seven, and nine through eleven, has not met either a minimum grade level competency or the minimum reading level as prescribed by the State Board of Education for the previous grade, the student shall be either retained in the current grade or enrolled in an appropriate reading assistance program as part of his or her instructional program. These provisions may not be responsible solely for withholding grade advancement more than once in grades two through seven. All students except the moderate and the severely and profoundly intellectually limited in grades three, seven, and nine through eleven shall be included.

(b) The State Board of Education shall promulgate bylaws to make effective this program by July 1, 1977 (1976, Chapter 767; 1977, Chapter 559.)


## MASSACHUSETTS

69:9—9.    Classes for illiterates and foreigners

The department, with the cooperation of any town applying therefor, may provide for such instruction in the use of English for persons eighteen years of age or over unable to speak, read or write the same, and in the fundamental principles of government and other subjects adapted to fit for American citizenship, as shall jointly be approved by the local school committee and the department. Schools and classes established therefor may be held in public school buildings, in industrial establishments or in such other places as may be approved in like manner. Teachers and supervisors employed therein by a town shall be chosen and their compensation fixed by the school committee, subject to the approval of the department.


71:1—1.    Maintenance, double sessions, subjects of instruction

Every town shall maintain, for at least the number of days required by the board of education in each school year unless specifically exempted as to any one year by said board, a sufficient number of schools for the instruction of all children who may legally attend a public school therein. No town shall hold double sessions in any public school, if in any other public school of comparable grade levels in such town there are vacant spaces for more than thirty-five children, the number of such vacant spaces to be computed without exceeding a maximum of thirty-five children to a classroom. The board of education may suspend the application of the preceding sentence in a particular town for a limited period. Such schools shall be taught by teachers of competent ability and good morals, and shall give instruction and training in orthography, reading, writing, the English language and grammar, geography, arithmetic, drawing, music, the history and constitution of the United States, the duties of citizenship, physiology and hygiene, physical education, and good behavior. In connection with physiology and hygiene, instruction as to the effects of alcoholic drinks and of stimulants and narcotics on the human system, and as to tuberculosis and its prevention, shall be given to all pupils in all schools under public control, except schools maintained solely for instruction in particular branches. Such other subjects as the school committee considers expedient may be taught in the public schools.

71:18—18.   Evening schools

Any town may, and every town in which there are issued during any year certificates authorizing the employment of twenty or more persons who do not possess the educational qualifications enumerated in section one of chapter seventy-six, shall maintain for not less than forty evenings during the following school year an evening school or schools for the instruction of persons over fourteen years of age in orthography, reading, writing, the English language and grammar, geography, arithmetic, industrial drawing, both free hand and mechanical, the history of the United States, physiology and hygiene and good behavior. Such other subjects may be taught as the school committee considers expedient.

## MICHIGAN

340:811   Education of aliens and illiterates, instruction in the English language and government

Section 811: The superintendent of public instruction is hereby authorized, with the cooperation of the boards of the school districts of this state, to provide for the education of aliens and of native illiterates over the age of 18 years residing in said districts, who are unable to read, write and speak the English language and who are unlearned in the principles of the government of this state and the United States. All instruction given under the provisions of this act shall be in the English language and shall be conducted by persons whose general qualifications and training are approved by the superintendent of public instruction.

## MINNESOTA

No code provisions found.

## MISSISSIPPI

37:13:11.    Required curriculum of grammar schools

The curriculum of the grammar schools shall consist of spelling, reading, arithmetic, geography, English grammar, composition, literature, United States history, history of Mississippi, elements of agriculture and forestry, civil government with special reference to the State of Mississippi and local government, physiology, hygiene with special reference to the effect of alcohol and narcotics on the human system, home and community sanitation, general science, and such other subjects as may be added by the state board of education.

The subject of safety shall be taught in the grammar school grades of all schools in the State of Mississippi, and the state textbook purchasing board shall prescribe the course to be taught and may, in its discretion, purchase such books as may be necessary for the teaching of said course.

37-3-47    State program of educational accountability and assessment of performance, duties of district school boards

The school board of every district in this state shall:

(a) Adopt a plan for a local accountability program designed to measure the adequacy and efficiency of educational programs offered by the school district in accordance with recommendations and criteria promulgated by the state department of education. The school board may appoint a broadly constituted citizen advisory accountability committee to make recommendations to the board relative to the program of educational accountability, but it shall be the sole responsibility of the district school board to implement plans required under this section.

(b) Report periodically to the residents of the school districts and the state department of education, in such form and giving such information as the state department of education requires, on the extent to which the school district has achieved the goals and objectives of its adopted plans.

37-3-43    State program of educational accountability and assessment of performance, declaration of purpose

(1) The legislature hereby declares that the purpose of sections 37-3-43 to 37-3-47 is to initiate and maintain a state program of educational

accountability and assessment of performance by the state department of education which will obtain and provide meaningful information to the citizens about the public elementary and secondary education schools in this state. This information about educational performance should relate to educational goals adopted by the department to student achievement in areas of the school curriculum, and to investigation of meaningful relationships within this performance.

(2) The legislature further declares that public school districts shall participate in the state accountability and assessment program and adopt compatible district plans in order to achieve improved educational accountability and to report meaningful information and results to the public.

37-3-45    State program of educational accountability and assessment of performance, duties of state department of education

(1) The state department of education shall develop a state accountability and assessment program which will:

(a) Establish a procedure for the continuing examination and updating of adoped state goals for elementary and secondary education.

(b) Identify goal-related performance objectives that will lead toward achieving stated goals.

(c) Establish procedures for evaluating the state's and school district's performance in relation to stated goals and objectives. Appropriate instruments to measure and evaluate progress shall be used to evaluate student performance.

(2) The state's program shall provide for an annual review which shall include assessing the performance of students in at least the public elementary and secondary schools in such areas of knowledge, skills, attitudes and understandings, and other characteristics or variables that will aid in identifying relationships and differentials in the level of educational performance that may exist between schools and school districts in the state.

(3) The state department of education shall:

(a) Promulgate rules for the implementation of this section.

(b) Enter into such contracts as may be necessary to carry out its duties and responsibilities under this section.

(c) Establish recommendations for components of school district accountability programs and provide technical assistance to school districts in planning and implementing their plans.

(d) Provide in-service training for personnel who will be involved in carrying out the state's program of educational accountability and assessment of performance.

(e) Monitor periodically the assessment and evaluation of programs implemented by school districts and make recommendations for their improvement and increased effectiveness.

(f) Annually report and make recommendations to the governor and legislature, the state board of education, school boards, and the general public on its findings with regard to the performance of the state elementary and secondary education school system.

(4) The state department of education may establish a state advisory committee on educational accountability to make recommendations and assist it in carrying out its responsibilities under this section.

37-23-121    Citation of law

Sections 37-23-11 through 37-23-131 shall be cited as the Mississippi Learning Resources Law of 1974.

37-23-123    Legislative intent

The intent of the legislature of the State of Mississippi, by passage of sections 37-23-121 through 37-23-131, is to develop and make available to children of this state who are experiencing learning problems or show evidence of potential learning problems a comprehensive program of services that will raise the quality of education for all children in the State of Mississippi who are in need of such services.

The intent of the legislature is not to displace existing screening teams but to organize, mobilize, and coordinate existing resources in the state for diagnostic services, while going into remote areas and rural sections where such resources are not available or within reasonable proximity. This service is intended to complement the services presently available from the state department of education and other agencies.

MISSOURI

No code provisions found.

## MONTANA

75-7512   Definitions of adult education and adult basic education

As used in this title, unless the context clearly indicates otherwise:

(a) the term "adult education" means the instruction of persons 16 years of age or older who are not regularly enrolled, full time pupils for the purposes of ANB computation; and

(b) the term "adult basic education" means instruction in basic skills such as reading, writing, arithmetic, and other skills required to function in society offered to persons 16 years of age or older who are not regularly enrolled, full-time pupils for the purposes of ANB computation. Adult basic education may include any subject normally offered in the basic curricula of an accredited elementary or secondary school in the state. Neither definition may include the instruction in postsecondary vocational technical centers.

## NEBRASKA

No code provisions found.

## NEW HAMPSHIRE

No code provisions found.

## NEW JERSEY

18A:7A-4.   Goal of free public schools

The goal of a thorough and efficient system of free public schools shall be to provide to all children in New Jersey, regardless of socio-economic status or geographic location, the educational opportunity which will prepare them to function politically, economically and socially in a democratic society.

18A:7A-5.  Major elements, guidelines

A thorough and efficient system of free public schools shall include the following major elements, which shall serve as guidelines for the achievement of the legislative goal and the implementation of this act:

a. Establishment of educational goals at both the State and local levels;

b. Encouragement of public involvement in the establishment of educational goals;

c. Instruction intended to produce the attainment of reasonable levels of proficiency in the basic communications and computational skills;

d. A breadth of program offerings designed to develop the individual talents and abilities of pupils;

e. Programs and supportive services for all pupils, especially those who are educationally disadvantaged or who have special educational needs;

f. Adequately equipped, sanitary and secure physical facilities and adequate materials and supplies;

g. Qualified instructional and other personnel;

h. Efficient administrative procedures;

i. An adequate state program of research and development; and

j. Evaluation and monitoring programs at both the State and local levels.

18A:7A-6.  State board, establishment of goals, standards, and rules

The State board, after consultation with the commissioner and review by the Joint Committee on the Public Schools shall (a) establish goals and standards which shall be applicable to all public schools in the State, including uniform Statewide standards of pupil proficiency in basic communications and computational skills at appropriate points in the educational careers of the pupils of the State, which standards of proficiency shall be reasonably related to those levels of proficiency ultimately necessary as part of the preparations of individuals to function politically, economically and socially in a democratic society, and which shall be consistent with the goals and guidelines established pursuant to sections 4 and 5 of this act, and (b) make rules concerning procedures for the establishment of particular educational goals, objectives and standards by local boards of education.

18A:7A-7.     Local boards of education, establishment of goals and standards, basic skills improvement plan

Each local board of education shall establish particular educational goals, objectives and standards pursuant to rules prescribed by the State board. In each district in which there are pupils whose proficiency in basic communications and computational skills is below the Statewide standard, the local board annually shall establish an interim goal designed to assure reasonable progress toward the goal of achievement by each such pupil of at least the Statewide standard of proficiency. Each such district as part of its annual educational plan, shall develop a basic skills improvement plan for progress toward such interim goal. Any such improvement plan shall be approved by the commissioner, and may include (a) curricular changes; (b) in-service training programs for teacher; (c) diagnostic, remedial, or skill-maintenance programs for pupils; (d) consultations with parents or guardians; (e) any other measure designed to promote progress toward such interim goal. Each year each district shall evaluate pupil proficiency in such other means as the board deems proper to determine pupil status and needs, ensure pupil progress, and assess the degree to which the goals have been achieved.

18A:7A-8.     Review and update of state goals and standards

The State board after consultation with the commissioner and review by the Joint Committee on the Public Schools shall, from time to time, but at least once every 5 years, review and update the State goals and standards established pursuant to this act. In reviewing and updating these goals and standards, the State board shall consult with, and be assisted by, (a) the Commissioner of Labor and Industry who, in consultation with employer and employee groups, shall report annually to the State board projecting labor needs and describing employment qualifications in New Jersey, (b) the Chancellor of Higher Education who, in consultation with the institutions of higher education in the State, shall report annually to the State board on entry requirements and anticipated enrollment levels, (c) the Commissioner of Health who shall report annually to the State board on current and projected health needs in New Jersey, (d) the Commissioner of Institutions and Agencies who shall report annually to the State board on the education of pupils under the jurisdiction of the department, and (e) such other employees and officers of the State as may be able to assist the State board in its activities pursuant to this section.

18A:7A-9.    Comprehensive needs assessment program, results, publicity

The commissioner, in cooperation with local school districts, shall from time to time, but at least once every 5 years, direct a comprehensive needs assessment program of all pupils in the State in light of State goals and standards, and shall make the results of the needs assessment program available to local school districts, which districts shall review and update their particular educational goals, objectives and standards to meet those needs. All such results shall be made public.

18A:7A-10.    Evaluation of performance of each school

For the purpose of evaluating the thoroughness and efficiency of all the public schools of the State, the commissioner, with the approval of the State board and after review of the Joint Committee of the Public Schools, shall develop and administer a uniform, Statewide system for evaluating the performance of each school. Such a system shall be based in part on annual testing for achievement in basic skill areas, and in part on such other means as the commissioner deems proper in order to (a) determine pupil status and needs, (b) ensure pupil progress, and (c) assess the degree to which the educational objectives have been achieved.

18A:7A-11.    Annual report of local school district, contents, annual report of commissioner, report on improvement of basic skills

Each school district shall make an annual report of its progress in conforming to the goals, objectives and standards developed pursuant to this act. Each district's annual report shall include but not be limited to:

a. Demographic data related to each school;

b. Results of assessment programs, including Statewide and district testing conducted at each school, and the result of the district evaluation of pupil proficiency in basic communication and computional skills;

c. Information on each school's fiscal operation, including the budget of each school;

d. Results of each school's effectiveness in achieving State, district, and school goals and objectives applicable to the pupils, including the effectiveness of any "basic skills improvement plan";

e. Plans and programs for professional improvement;

f. Plans to carry out innovative or experimental educational programs designed to improve the quality of education; and

g. Recommendations for school improvements during the ensuing year.

h. Additionally, the State Board of Education may from time to time require each district to submit a facilities survey, including current use practices and projected capital project needs, but not more frequently than once every 2 years.

The district reports shall be submitted to the commissioner by July 1 of each year and he shall make them the basis for an annual report to the Governor and the Legislature, describing the condition of education in New Jersey, the efforts of New Jersey schools in meeting the standards of a thorough and efficient education, the steps underway to correct deficiencies in schools in comparison to other state education systems in the United States.

In addition to such annual report the commissioner shall, 4 years from the effective date of this amendatory act, report to the Governor and the Joint Committee on the Public Schools assessing the effectiveness of this amendatory act in improving the proficiency of the pupils of this State in basic communications and computational skills. Within 6 months of receiving such report the Joint Committee on the Public Schools shall recommend to the Legislature any necessary or desirable changes or modifications in this amendatory act.

18A:7A-12   Comprehensive report of state board, contents

In addition to the annual reports required by section 11 of this act, the State board shall, 4 years after the effective date of this act, make a comprehensive report to the Governor and the Legislature assessing the effectiveness of this act in producing a thorough and efficient system of free public schools. The report shall include an account of the progress of each local school district in meeting the goals, objectives and standards prescribed under sections 6 and 7 of this act, identify those districts and schools which fail to meet them and make recommendations, if necessary, for hastening the elimination of any deficiencies.

18A:7A-13   Governor's biennial message to Legislature

Thereafter, the Governor shall deliver a biennial message to the Legislature on the progress of New Jersey's schools in providing a thorough and efficient education and recommending legislative action, if appropriate.

18A:7A-14    Failure of school or school district to show progress, remedial plan, insufficiency, corrective actions, hearing on order to show cause

The commissioner shall review the results of the evaluations conducted and reports submitted pursuant to sections 10 and 11 of this act. If the commissioner shall find that a school or a school district has failed to show sufficient progress toward the goals, guidelines, objectives and standards, including the State goal and any local interim goal concerning pupil proficiency in basic communications and computational skills, established in and pursuant to this act, he shall advise the local board of education of such determination, and shall direct that a remedial plan be prepared and submitted to him for approval. If the commissioner approves the plan, he shall assure its implementation in a timely and effective manner. If the commissioner finds that the remedial plan prepared by the local board of education is insufficient, he shall order the local board to show cause why the corrective actions provided in section 15 of the act should not be utilized. The hearing upon said order to show cause shall be conducted in the manner prescribed by subdivision B of article 2 of chapter 6 of Title 18A of the New Jersey Statutes.

18A:7A-15    Corrective actions, administrative order specifying remedial plan to local board

If, after a plenary hearing, the commissioner determines that it is necessary to take corrective action, he shall have the power to order necessary budgetary changes within the school district, to order in-service training programs for teachers and other school personnel, or both. If he determines that such corrective actions are insufficient, he shall have the power to recommend to the State board that it take appropriate action. The State board, on determining that the school district is not providing a thorough and efficient education, notwithstanding any other provision of law to the contrary, shall have the power to issue an administrative order specifying a remedial plan to the local board of education, which plan may include budgetary changes or other measures the State board determines to be appropriate. Nothing herein shall limit the right of any party to appeal the administrative order to the Superior Court.

18A:7A-16    Failure or refusal to comply with administrative order, application to court for order directing compliance

Should the local board of education fail or refuse to comply with an administrative order issued pursuant to section 15 of this act, the

State board shall apply to the Superior Court by a proceeding in lieu of prerogative writ for an order directing the local school board to comply with such administrative order.


## NEW YORK

65:3204—3a.  Courses of study

(1) The course of study for the first eight years of full time public day schools shall provide for instruction in at least the twelve common school branches of arithmetic, reading, spelling, writing, the English language, geography, United States history, civics, hygiene, physical training, the history of New York state and science.


4105    Required attendance upon instruction

1. Every Indian child between six and sixteen years of age in proper physical and mental condition to attend school, shall regularly attend upon instruction at a school in which at least the common school branches of reading, spelling, writing, arithmetic, English grammar and geography are taught in English or upon equivalent instruction by a competent teacher elsewhere than at such school as follows: Every Indian child between fourteen and sixteen years of age not regularly and lawfully engaging in any useful employment or service, and every such child between six and fourteen years of age, shall so attend upon instruction as many days annually during the period between the first days of September and the following July as a public school of the community or district of the reservation, in which such child resides, shall be in session during the same period.

2. If any such child shall so attend upon instruction elsewhere than at the public school, such instruction shall be at least equivalent to the instruction given to Indian children of like age at a school of the community or district in which such child shall reside; and such attendance shall be for at least as many hours of each day thereof, as required of children of like age at public schools and no greater total amount of holidays and vacations shall be deducted from such attendance during the period such attendance is required than is allowed in public schools for children of like age. Occasional absences from such attendance not amounting to irregular attendance in a fair meaning of the term, shall be allowed upon such excuses only as would be allowed in like cases by the general rules and practices of public schools.

3. Transportation shall be provided for Indian children who live more than a mile from the elementary and high schools they attend,

and the commissioner of education is hereby empowered to make provision for the cost of the same as a part of the care and education of Indian children.


NORTH CAROLINA


Article 39A:
High School Competency Testing

Section 115-320.6     Purpose

The State Board of Education shall adopt tests or other measurement devices which may be used to assure that the graduates of the public high schools and graduates of nonpublic high schools supervised by the State Board of Education pursuant to the provisions of Article 32 of Chapter 115 of the General Statutes possess those skills and that knowledge necessary to function independently and successfully in assuming the responsibilities of citizenship. This Article has three purposes: (i) to assure that all high school graduates possess those minimum skills and that knowledge thought necessary to function as a member of society, (ii) to provide a means of identifying strengths and weaknesses in the education process, and (iii) to establish additional means for making the education system accountable to the public for results.


Section 115-320.7     Competency Test Commission

(a) The Governor shall appoint a Competency Test Commission on or before July 1, 1977, which shall be composed of 15 members who shall hold office for four years or until their successors are appointed. Any vacancy on the Competency Test Commission shall be filled by the Governor for the unexpired term. Five members of the Competency Test Commission shall be persons serving as teachers or principals in high schools; five shall be citizens of the State interested in education; two shall be professional educators from the facilities of institutions of higher education in the State; two shall be persons competent in the field of psychological measurement; and one shall be the superintendent of a local administrative unit in the State. The members shall be entitled to compensation for each day spent on the work of the Competency Test Commission as approved by the State Board of Education and receive reimbursement for travel and subsistence expenses incurred in the performance of their duties at rates specified in G.S. 138-5 or 138-6, whichever is applicable to the individual member. All currently employed teachers serving on the Commission shall be entitled to receive full pay for each day spent on the work of the Commission without any reduction in salary for a substitute teacher's pay.

(b) The Superintendent of Public Instruction, or his designee, shall serve as an *ex officio*, nonvoting member of the Competency Test Commission.

Section 115-320.8    Duties of Commission

(a) No later than January 1, 1978, the Competency Test Commission shall recommend to the State Board of Education tests or other measuring devices that may be used to measure those skills and that knowledge thought necessary to enable an individual to function independently and successfully in assuming the responsibilities of citizenship.

(b) After tests have been approved by the State Board of Education and administered, for informational and research purposes only, to all eleventh grade students in the public and nonpublic high schools of the State during the spring semester of 1978, the Competency Test Commission shall review the summaries of these test results.

(c) No later than July 1, 1978, the Competency Test Commission shall provide the State Board of Education with written recommendations as to the adoption of the tests that were administered for research and informational purposes and as to the minimum levels of performance that it believes should be expected of graduating high school seniors.

(d) After the adoption of tests and minimum graduation standards by the State Board of Education, the tests shall be administered annually to all eleventh grade students in the public schools beginning in the fall of 1978. Students who fail to attain the required minimum standard for graduation in the eleventh grade shall be given remedial instruction and additional opportunities to take the test up to and including the last month of the twelfth grade. Students who fail to pass parts of the test shall be retested on only those parts they fail. Students in the eleventh grade who are enrolled in special education programs or who have been officially designated as eligible for participation in such programs may be excluded from the testing programs.

(e) The Competency Test Commission shall annually advise the State Board of Education on matters pertaining to the use of high school graduation competency tests.

## ARTICLE 39B:
### Statewide Testing Program

Section 115-320.19    Purpose

In order to assess the effectiveness of the educational process, and to insure that each pupil receives the maximum educational process, the State Board of Education shall implement an annual statewide testing program in basic subjects. It is the intent of this testing program to help local school systems and teachers identify and correct student needs in basic skills rather than to provide a tool for comparison of individual students or to evaluate teacher performance. The first statewide testing program shall be conducted prior to the end of the 1977-78 school year for the first, second, third, sixth and ninth grades, provided that criterion reference tests shall be used in the first and second grades and norm reference tests shall be used in the testing program in grades three, six and nine. Students in these grade levels who are enrolled in special education programs or who have been officially designated as eligible for participation in such programs may be excluded from the testing programs.

Section 115-320.20    State Board of Education responsibilities

The State Board of Education shall have the responsibility and authority to make those policies necessary for the implementation of the intent and purposes of this Article, not inconsistent with the provisions of this Article.

Section 115-320.21    Appointment of Testing Commission

(a) On or before July 1, 1977, the Governor shall appoint a Testing Commission composed of 11 nominated and appointed. Any vacancy on the Testing Commission shall be filled by the Governor by appointment for the unexpired term. Six of the members of the Testing Commission shall be certified teachers currently employed for the grades in which tests are to be administered; two shall be persons competent in the field of psychological measurement; one shall be a school principal; one shall be a supervisor of elementary instruction; and one shall be the superintendent of a local administrative unit. The members of the Testing Commission shall be entitled to compensation for each day spent on the work of the Testing Commission, as approved by the State Board of Education, and receive reimbursement for travel and subsistence expense incurred in the performance of their duties at the rates specified in G.S. 138-5 or 138-6, whichever is applicable to the individual member. All currently employed teachers serving on the Commission shall be entitled to receive their full pay for each school day spent on the work of the Commission without any reduction in salary for a substitute teacher's pay.

(b) The Superintendent of Public Instruction, or his designee, shall serve as an *ex officio*, nonvoting member of the Testing Commission.

Section 115-320.22     Evaluation and selection of tests

(a) The members of the Testing Commission shall secure copies of tests designed to measure the level of academic achievement. Each of these tests shall be examined carefully and the Testing Commission shall file with the State Board of Education, a written evaluation of each of these tests along with appropriate recommendations. In evaluating a test, the Testing Commission shall give special consideration to the suitability of a test to the instructional level or special education program or level for which it is intended to be used and the validity of the test.

(b) The Testing Commission shall annually review the suitability and validity of the tests in use by the State Board of Education for the purposes of this Article and investigate the suitability and validity of other tests. A written evaluation of all tests and any recommendations considered by the Testing Commission shall be filed with the State Board of Education.

# NORTH DAKOTA

15:59:07     Contracts for handicapped children to attend private schools

If any school district in this state has any educable elementary or high school student who in the opinion of a qualified psychologist, a medical doctor and the district superintendent is unable to attend the public school in the district, which has proper facilities for the education of such student, if there are no public schools in the state with the necessary facilities which will accept such student. No school district shall enter into a contract with any private nonsectarian nonprofit corporation for the education of any student having a physical handicap or learning disability, unless the curriculum provided by such school and the contract has been approved in advance by the superintendent of public instruction. The contract shall provide that such school district agrees to pay to the private nonsectarian nonprofit corporation as part of the cost of educating such student an amount for the school year equal to three times the state average per pupil elementary or high school cost, depending on whether the enrollment would be in a grade or high school department, provided that such payment shall not exceed the actual per-pupil cost incurred by such private, nonsectarian nonprofit corporation. The district of the student's residence shall be reimbursed from funds appropriated by the legislative assembly for the foundation aid program, in an amount equal to sixty percent of the payment made to such private, nonsectarian nonprofit corporation. If the attendance of such student at such school is for less than a school year, then the contract shall provide for such lesser amount prorated on a monthly basis. The reimbursement herein provided to the contracting district from the foundation aid program shall be in lieu of any other foundation aid to which the district might otherwise be entitled.

As used in this section, the term "learning disability" shall mean a disorder in one or more of the basic psychological processes involved in understanding or in using spoken or written languages, and which may be manifested in disorders of listening, thinking, talking, reading, writing, spelling, or arithmetic. The term "learning disability" shall include, but not be limited to, such conditions as perceptual handicaps, brain injury, minimal brain dysfunction, dyslexia, and developmental aphasia, but shall not include learning problems due primarily to visual, hearing or motor handicaps, mental retardation, emotional disturbance, or environmental disadvantage.

15:38:07     Required subjects in the public schools

The following subjects shall be taught in the public schools to pupils who are sufficiently advanced to pursue the same: spelling, reading, writing, arithmetic, language, English grammar, geography, United States history, civil government, nature study, and elements of agriculture. Physiology and hygiene also shall be taught, and in teaching such subject, the teacher shall:

1. Give special and thorough instruction concerning the nature of alcoholic drinks and narcotics and their effect upon the human system;

2. Give simple lessons in the nature, treatment, and prevention of tuberculosis and other contagious and infectious diseases;

3. Give, to all pupils below the high school and above the third year of school work, not less than four lessons in hygiene each week for ten weeks of each school year from textbooks adapted to the grade of the pupils;

4. Give, to all pupils in the three lowest primary school years, not less than three oral lessons on hygiene each week for ten weeks of

each school year, using textbooks adapted to the grade of the pupils as guides or standards for such instruction.

## OHIO

**3313:60    Courses of study required**

Boards of education of county, exempted village, and city school districts shall prescribe a graded course of study for all schools under their control subject to the approval of the state board of education. In such graded courses of study there shall be included the study of the following subjects:

(A) The language arts, including reading, writing, spelling, oral and written English, and literature;

(B) Geography, the history of the United States and of Ohio and national, state and local government in the United States;

(C) Mathematics;

(D) Natural science, including instruction in the conservation of natural resources;

(E) Health and physical education, which shall include instruction in the harmful effects, and legal restrictions against the use of drugs of abuse, alcoholic beverages, and tobacco;

(F) The fine arts including music;

(G) First aid, safety and fire prevention.

Every school shall include in the requirements for promotion from the eighth grade to the ninth grade one year's course of study of American history.

Every high school shall include in the requirements for graduation from any curriculum one unit of American history and government, including a study of the constitutions of the United States and of Ohio.

Basic instruction in geography, United States history, the government of the United States, the government of the state of Ohio, local government in Ohio, the Declaration of Independence, the United States Constitution and the Constitution of the state of Ohio shall be required before pupils may participate in courses involving the study of social problems, economics, foreign affairs, United Nations, world government, socialism and communism.

## OKLAHOMA

**11:103    Courses of study**

Courses of study formulated, prescribed, adopted or approved by the State Board of Education for the instruction of pupils in the public schools of the state shall include such courses as are necessary to insure:

1. The teaching of citizenship in the United States, in the State of Oklahoma, and other countries, through the study of the ideals, history and government of the United States, other countries of the world, and the State of Oklahoma and through the study of the principles of democracy as they apply in the lives of citizens;

2. The teaching of health, physical fitness, and safety through the study of proper diet, the effects of alcoholic beverages, narcotics and other substances on the human system and through the study of such other subjects as will promote healthful living and help to establish proper health habits in the lives of school children; and through training in the driving and operation of motor vehicles and such other devices of transportation as may be desirable and other aspects of safety which will promote the reduction of accidents and encourage habits of safe living among school children;

3. The teaching of the necessary basic skills of learning and communication, including reading, writing, the use of numbers and such other skills as may be necessary for efficiency in the normal process of living;

4. The teaching of the conservation of natural resources of the state and the nation that are necessary and desirable to sustain life and contribute to the comfort and welfare of the people now living and those who will live here in the future, such as soil, water, forests, minerals, oils, gas, all forms of wildlife, both plant and animal, and such other natural resources as may be considered desirable to study;

5. The teaching of vocational education, by the study of the various aspects of agriculture, through courses and farm youth organizations, such as FFA and 4-H Clubs, homemaking and home economics, trades and industries, distributive education, mechanical and industrial arts and such other aspects of vocational education as will promote occupational competence among school children and adults as potential and actual citizens of the state and nation:

6. The teaching of such other aspects of human living and citizenship as will achieve the legitimate objectives and purposes of public education.

336.079    Special English courses for certain children

Specific courses to teach speaking, reading, and writing of the English language shall be provided at each grade level, starting at first grade, to those children who are unable to profit from classes taught in English. Such courses shall be taught to such a level in school or may be required until children are able to profit from classes conducted in English.


PENNSYLVANIA


15:1511    Subjects of instruction, flag code

In every elementary public and private school, established and maintained in this Commonwealth, the following subjects shall be taught, in the English language and from English texts: English, including spelling, reading and writing, arithmetic, geography, the history of the United States and of Pennsylvania, civics including loyalty to the State and National Government, safety education, and the humane treatment of birds and animals, health, including physical education, and physiology, music and art. Other subjects shall be taught in the public elementary schools and also in the public high schools as may be prescribed by the standards of the State Board of Education. All such subjects, except foreign languages, shall be taught in the English language and from English texts. Provided, however, that, at the discretion of the Superintendent of Public Instruction, the teaching of subjects in a language other than English may be permitted as part of a sequence in foreign language study or as part of a bilingual education program if the teaching personnel are properly certified in the subject fields. Each school district shall provide and distribute to each pupil, enrolled in the eighth grade of the public schools, one illustrated copy of the National Flag Code, and shall, from time to time, make available such copies as are necessary for replacements from year to year. It shall be the duty of each teacher in the public schools to make such use of the code as may, from time to time, seem proper.


24:1776    Professors and assistants in certain courses of study (refers to normal schools)

Each school shall have at least six professors of liberal education and known ability in their respective departments, namely: One of orthography, reading and elocution; one of writing, drawing and book-keeping; one of arithmetic, and the higher branches of mathematics; one of geography and history; one of grammar and English literature, and one of theory and practice of teaching, together with such tutors and assistants therein, and such professors of natural mental and moral science, languages and literature, as the condition of the school and the number of students may require.

## RHODE ISLAND

16:29:1    Establishment of free evening schools

One or more public evening schools, in which attendance shall be free for persons resident in the town in which such school shall be located, and in which the speaking, reading and writing of the English language shall be taught for two (2) hours on each of at least one hundred (100) nights between the first of September and the first of June in each year, shall be established and maintained by the school committee of every town in which twenty (20) or more persons more than sixteen (16) and less than twenty-one (21) years of age, who cannot speak, read and write the English language, are resident; provided, that the school committee of two (2) adjoining towns may unite for the purpose of establishing and maintaining jointly, at some convenient place, an evening school for persons resident in such towns.

## SOUTH CAROLINA

21:411    Required subjects

The county board of education and the board of trustees for each school district shall see that in every school under their care there shall be taught, as far as practicable, orthography, reading, writing, arithmetic, geography, English grammar, the elements of agriculture, the history of the United States and of this State, the principles of the Constitutions of the United States and of this State, morals and good behavior, algebra, physiology and hygiene (especially as to the effects of alcoholic liquors and narcotics upon the human system), English literature and such other branches as the State Board may from time to time direct.

## SOUTH DAKOTA

No code provisions found.

## TENNESSEE

49:1901     Elementary school curriculum

The course of study in all public elementary schools shall embrace the following subjects: spelling, reading, writing, arithmetic, grammar, geography, history of Tennessee containing the Constitution of the state, history of the United States containing the Constitution of the United States, hygiene and sanitation, physical education, vocal music and drawing. Instruction in hygiene and sanitation shall include the nature of alcoholic drinks, narcotics, and smoking of cigarettes, and their effects upon the human system. Said course shall be divided into eight (8) grades, each grade representing a year's work as outlined in the course of study prepared under the direction of the state commissioner of education.

49:1902     City elementary school curriculum

In every city elementary school there shall be taught reading, writing, spelling, arithmetic, English grammar, geography, Tennessee history, United States history containing the Constitution of the United States, hygiene and sanitation, music, drawing, and such other subjects as the city board of education may require.

## TEXAS

16:04     (b) Notwithstanding the provisions of Subsection (a) of this section, the program of preschool education shall be extended first to "educationally handicapped" children as preparation for the regular school program in which such children will participate in subsequent years. For purposes of this section, a child is "educationally handicapped" if he cannot speak, read, and comprehend the English language or if he is from a family whose income, according to standards promulgated by the State Board of Education, is at or below a subsistence level. The program shall include an appreciation for the cultural and familial traditions of the child's parents and also an awareness and appreciation of the broader world in which the child must live; assist the child in developing appropriate language skills; prepare the child to participate in the world of his peers and the broader cultural stream into which he will progressively move as he matures; begin the development of the mental and physical skills and cooperative attitudes needed for adequate performance in a school setting; and begin the development of his unique character and personality traits.

16:104   Comprehensive special education program for exceptional children

(a) It is the intention of this section to provide for a comprehensive special education program for exceptional children in Texas.

(b) As used in this section:

(1) "Exceptional children" means children between the ages of 3 and 21, inclusive, with educational handicaps (physical, retarded, emotionally disturbed, and/or children with language and/or learning disabilities) as hereinafter more specifically defined; autistic children; and children leaving and not attending public school for a time because of pregnancy—disabilities which render regular services and classes of the public schools inconsistent with their educational needs.

(2) "Physically handicapped children" means children of educable mind whose body functions or members are so impaired from any cause that they cannot be adequately or safely educated in the regular classes of the public schools without the provision of special services.

(3) "Mentally retarded children" means children whose mental capacity is such that they cannot be adequately educated in the regular classes of the public schools without the provision of special services.

(4) "Handicapped children" means children who have physical or mental disabilities, singularly or in combination, that:

(A) cannot readily be corrected through routine medical services of a nonextended nature;
(B) for the children constitute or result in a substantial handicap to the deriving of benefits from regular classroom programs and routine school activities.

(5)"Language and/or learning disabled children" means children who are so deficient in the acquisition of language and/or learning skills including, but not limited to, the ability to reason, think, speak, read, write, spell, or to make mathematical calculations, as identified by educational and/or psychological and/or medical diagnosis that they must be provided special services for educational progress. The term "language and/or learning disabled children" shall also apply to children diagnosed as having specific development dyslexia.

(6) "Special services" required for the instruction of or program for exceptional children means special teaching in the public school curriculum inside and/or outside the regular classroom; corrective teaching, such as lipreading, speech correction, sight conservation corrective health habits; transportation, special seats, books, instructional media, and supplies; professional counseling with students and parents; supervision of professional services and pupil evaluation services; established teaching techniques for children with language and/or learning disabilities.

(c) Under rules, regulations, and/or formulas adopted by the State Board of Education subject to the provisions of this section, exceptional children teacher units, in addition to other professional and paraprofessional unit allotments herein authorized, shall be allotted to any eligible school district in the number determinable thereunder. Exceptional children teacher units for pupils who are both severely physically handicapped and mentally retarded shall be allocated on a separate formula from other type units.

(d) Professional personnel for the operation and maintenance of a program of special education shall be:

(1) exceptional children teachers;

(2) special education supervisors;

(3) special education counselors;

(4) special service teachers, such as itinerant teachers of the homebound and visiting teachers, whose duties may or may not be performed in whole or in part on the campus of any school; and

(5) psychologists and other pupil evaluation specialists. The minimum salary for such specialist to be used in computing salary allotment for purposes of this section shall be established by the commissioner of education.

(e) Paraprofessional personnel for the operation and maintenance of a program of special education shall consist of persons engaged as teacher aides, who may or may not hold a teacher certificate. The qualifications and minimum salary levels of paraprofessional personnel for salary allotment shall be established by the commissioner of education.

(f) Quantitative bases for the allotment of all special education unit personnel under Subsection (c) of this section shall be established by the commissioner of education under rules adopted by the State

Board of Education. Any school district, at its expense, may employ any special education personnel in excess of its state allotment and may supplement the minimum salary allotted by the state for any special education personnel, and any district is authorized at local expense to pay for all or part of further or continuing training or education of its special education personnel.

(g) Special education unit personnel may be employed and/or utilized on a full-time, part-time, or consultative basis, or may be allotted by the commissioner of education, pursuant to cooperative districts' agreement, jointly to serve two or more school districts. Two or more school districts may operate jointly their special education program and any school district may contract where feasible with any other school district for all or any part of the program of special education for the children of either district, under rules and regulations established by the commissioner of education.

(h) To each school district operating an approved special education program there shall also be allotted a special service allowance in an amount to be determined by the commissioner of education for pupil evaluation, special seats, books, instructional media, and other supplies required for quality instruction.

(i) The minimum monthly base pay and increments for teaching experience for an exceptional children teacher or a special service teacher conducting a 10, 11, or 12 months special education program approved by the commissioner of education shall be the same as that of a classroom teacher as provided in Subchapter B of this chapter; provided that special education teachers shall have qualifications approved by the commissioner of education. The annual salary of special education teachers shall be the monthly base salary, plus increments, multiplied by 10, 11, or 12 as applicable.

(j) The minimum monthly base pay and increments for teaching experience for special education counselors and supervisors engaged in a 10, 11, or 12 months special education program approved by the commissioner of education shall be the same as that of a counselor or supervisor as provided in Subchapter B of this chapter; provided that such counselors and supervisors shall have qualifications approved by the commissioner of education. The annual salary of special education counselors and supervisors shall be the monthly base salary, plus increments, multiplied by 10, 11, or 12 as applicable.

(k) The salary costs of special education teacher units, other professional and paraprofessional units authorized in Subsections (c), (d), and (e) of this section, and operating costs as provided in Subsection (h), computed as other costs of the Foundation School

Program for local fund assignment purposes, shall be paid from the Foundation Program School Fund. Provided further, that any school district may supplement any part of the comprehensive special education program it operates or participated in with funds or sources available to it from local sources, public and/or private.

(p) The State Board of Education shall adopt such policies and procedures for the administration of the comprehensive special education program for exceptional children in Texas as might be necessary to assure that:

(1) in the event that comprehensive special education services cannot be provided to all exceptional children, handicapped children throughout the State of Texas will be served first;

(2) the priority in services to handicapped children will be determined according to the severity of the handicaps of the children eligible for special education services; and

(3) sufficiently detailed records are kept and reports received to allow meaningful evaluation of the effectiveness of the policies and procedures adopted pursuant to this subsection.

(q) Special services extended to children who are handicapped by a hearing or visual impairment, or by both hearing and visual impairments, shall be provided by qualified staff certified by reputable public or private nonprofit organizations in the fields or work for the blind or work for the deaf as having the professional credentials and competencies required for certification within those fields.

21:101    Courses of study

All public free schools in this state shall be required to offer instruction in the following subjects: English grammar, reading in English, orthography, penmanship, composition, arithmetic, mental arithmetic, United States history, Texas history, modern geography, civil government, physiology and hygiene, physical education, and, in all grades, a course or courses in which some attention is given to the effects of alcohol and narcotics. Such subjects shall be taught in compliance with any applicable provision of this subchapter.

UTAH

53:27:3    Alien attendance

All aliens residing in this state, except those who may be physically or mentally disqualified, between the ages of 16 and 35 years, who do not possess such ability to speak, read and write the English language as is required for the completion of the fifth grade of the public schools, shall attend a public evening school class for at least four hours a week during the entire time an evening school class of the proper grade shall be in session in the district residence, or until the necessary ability has been acquired; provided, that regular attendance at a public day school or part-time school shall be accepted in place of attendance at an evening school class. The determination as to the persons subject to the provisions of this section shall be made by examination to be held under rules to be prescribed by the state board of education. The board of education of any school district or the state board of education may direct any aliens to take such examinations, except for good cause, shall be taken as evidence that they are subject to the provisions of this section.

## VERMONT

**16:906   Courses of study**

In the public schools learning experiences shall be provided for pupils adapted to their age and ability in the fields of:

(1) Basic skills of communication, including reading, writing, and the use of numbers;

(2) Citizenship, history, and government in Vermont and the United States;

(3) Physical education and principles of health with special reference to the effect of tobacco, alcoholic drinks, and drugs on the human system and on society;

(4) Knowledge of English, American and other literature;

(5) The natural sciences;

(6) Such other knowledge as the state board or a local school board may deem desirable.

## VIRGINIA

**22:233   Subjects taught in elementary grades**

In the elmentary grades of every public school the following subjects shall be taught: Spelling, reading, writing, arithmetic, grammar, geography, physiology and hygiene, drawing, civil government, history of the United States and history of Virginia.

Chapter 714 H 256:     An Act to revise the standard of quality for the several school divisions and to repeal Chapter 316 of the Acts of Assembly of 1974, relating to such standards of quality. Approved April 12, 1976

Whereas, Section 2 of Article VIII of the Constitution of Virginia provides that standards of quality for the several school divisions shall be determined and prescribed from time to time by the Board of Education, subject to revision only by the General Assembly; and

Whereas, the goals of public education in Virginia are to aid each pupil, consistent with his or her abilities and educational needs, to:

1. Become competent in the fundamental academic skills;

2. Be qualified for further education and/or employment;

3. Participate in society as a responsible citizen;

4. Develop ethical standards of behavior and a positive and realistic self-image;

5. Exhibit a responsibility for the enhancement of beauty in daily life;

6. Practice sound habits of personal health; and

Whereas, such Board has prescribed such standards and it is now the desire of the General Assembly that such standards be revised; now, therefore,

Be it enacted by the General Assembly of Virginia;

Section 1: That the standards of quality for public schools in Virginia, as determined and prescribed by the Board of Education, and effective July one, nineteen hundred seventy-six, and revised as follows:

## 1. Basic Learning Skills

A. The General Assembly concludes that one of the fundamental goals of public education must be to enable each student to achieve, to the best of his or her ability, certain basic skills. Each school division shall, therefore, give the highest priority in its instructional program to developing the reading, communications, and mathematics skills of all students, with concentrated effort in the primary (kindergarten through grade three) and intermediate (grades four through six ) grades. Remedial work shall begin for low achieving students upon identification of their needs.

B. By September, nineteen hundred seventy-eight, the Board of Education, in cooperation with the local school divisions, shall establish specific minimum Statewide educational objectives in reading, communications and mathematics skills that should be achieved during the primary grades and during the intermediate grades.

C. Each school division shall provide a kindergarten program of at least one-half day for all eligible children. Attendance in a kindergarten program shall be mandatory for each child of kindergarten age; provided that the parents or guardian of any child may decline to enroll that child in kindergarten or withdraw that child from kindergarten without prejudice, in which case attendance shall not be mandatory.

## 2. Career Preparation

A. The General Assembly concludes that a goal of public education must be to enable each student, upon leaving school, to continue successfully a program of advanced education or to enter the world of work. Each school division shall, therefore, by September, nineteen hundred seventy-eight, provide programs, approved by the Board of Education, that offer:

1. Career guidance to all secondary students:

2. Adequate preparation to secondary students planning to continue their education; and

3. Vocational education providing marketable skills for students who are not planning to continue their education beyond high school. Those students not completing their public school education should possess the basic skills and attitudes, commensurate with their capabilities, to obtain employment upon leaving school.

B. By June thirty, nineteen hundred seventy-seven, each school division, in cooperation with the Board of Education, shall have a plan for alternative career education to provide instructional choices for parents and students. By September, nineteen hundred eighty, each school division shall have a program of alternative career education.

C. Students enrolled in alternative education programs approved by the Board of Education shall be counted in the Average Daily Membership of the school division in which they would normally be enrolled. State funds received by a school division for students enrolled in alternative education programs shall be disbursed to the programs in proportion to the number of students actually enrolled therein, in accordance with guidelines established by the Board of Education and to the extent permitted by the Constitution and laws of Virginia.

### 3. Special Education

Each school division shall have a program, acceptable to the Board of Education, for early identification of students who may need special education. When handicapping conditions have been identified, such students shall be provided with a program of special education which is acceptable to the Board of Education.

### 4. Gifted and Talented

A. Each school division shall provide differentiated instruction to increase educational challenges and to enrich the experiences and opportunities available to gifted and talented students.

B. High school students who begin advanced education, whether academic or vocational, before graduating from high school, shall be awarded a high school diploma upon satisfactory completion of their first year of advanced education, in accordance with regulations prescribed by the Board of Education.

### 5. Personnel

A. Each school division shall employ with State basic school aid funds and local funds at least forty-eight professional personnel for each one thousand students in Average Daily Membership.

B. The maximum number of students in Average Daily Membership per certified classroom teacher for each first, second, or third grade classroom in all school divisions shall be as follows: for 1977-78, twenty-eight; for 1978-79, twenty-seven; for 1979-80, twenty-six; for 1980-81, twenty-five; and for 1981-82, no kindergarten classroom shall have more than twenty-five students in Average Daily Membership per certified classroom shall have more than twenty-four students in Average Daily Membership per certified teacher. If a full-time teacher's aide is assigned to a kindergarten through third grade class-room, the maximum student limit for that classroom shall be raised by seven.

C. Each school division shall provide a program of personnel develop-ment. This program shall be designed to help all personnel to become more proficient in performing their assigned responsibilities, includ-ing the identification of individuals with special instructional needs.

### 6. Teacher Preparation

A. Beginning with the 1981-82 school year, one certification require-ment for teachers beginning their teaching career shall be the successful completion of the equivalent of a five-year program of teacher prep-aration, at least the fifth year of which shall be a supervised teaching internship. The Board of Education is directed to develop the rules and regulations for the operation of this program.

B. After September, nineteen hundred seventy-eight, every certified teacher shall be required every five years to have his or her certificate renewed by a certification board. The Board of Education shall estab-lish general criteria for initial certification and certificate renewal. The courses and in-service training taken for certificate renewal shall be demonstrated as pertinent to the subject area in which the teacher now teaches or plans to teach.

### 7. Testing and Measurement

A. By September, nineteen hundred seventy-eight, each school divi-sion shall primarily utilize testing programs that will provide the individual classroom teacher with information to help in assessing the educational needs of individual students.

B. Beginning in September, nineteen hundred seventy-eight, each school division shall annually administer uniform Statewide tests developed by the Department of Education to measure the extent to which each student in that division has progressed during the last year in achieving the specific educational objectives that have been established under Standard 1-B.

### 8. Accreditation

Each school division shall develop by July one of the next school year a plan acceptable to the Board of Education to meet accrediting standards for any school that is unaccredited or accredited with a warning by the Board of Education. The chairman and members of any evaluation committee on which accreditation is based shall be independent of the school division and they shall be selected by the Superintendent of Public Instruction. All accreditation reports shall be open for public instruction.

### 9. Planning and Public Involvement

Each school division shall involve the staff and community in revising and extending biennially a six-year school improvement plan. This plan shall be reviewed and approved by the local school board and submitted by July one of each even year to the Superintendent of Public Instruction for approval by the Board of Education. This plan shall include:

1. The measurable objectives of the school division stated in terms of student performance;

2. An assessment of the extent to which the objectives are being achieved, including follow-up studies of former students;

3. Strategies for achieving the objectives of the school division; and

4. Evidence of community participation in the development of the six year plan.

A report shall be made by November one of each even year to the local school board and to the public on the extent to which the measurable objectives of the preceding two school years were achieved. Deviations from the plan shall be explained.

### 10. Policy Manual

Each school division shall maintain an up-to-date policy manual which shall include:

1. A grievance procedure prescribed, and amended from time to time as deemed necessary, by the Board of Education;

2. A system of direct communication between the local school board and its employees, along guidelines established or approved by the Board of Education, whereby the views of school employees may be received in an orderly and constructive manner in matters of concern to them; and

3. A cooperatively developed procedure for personnel evaluation.

An up-to-date copy of the school division policy manual shall be kept in the library of each school in that division and shall be available to the employees and to the public.

Section 2. The standards of quality prescribed above shall be the only standards of quality required by Section 2 of Article VIII of the Constitution of Virginia.

Section 3. School divisions providing programs and services, as provided in the standards of quality prescribed above, with State basic and local funds may be required to provide such services and programs only to an extent proportionate to the funding therefor provided by the General Assembly.

# WASHINGTON

28A:05:010     Common school curriculum, fundamentals in conduct

All common schools shall give instruction in reading, penmanship, orthography, written and mental arithmetic, geography, English grammar, physiology and hygiene with special reference to the effects of alcoholic stimulants and narcotics on the human system, the history of the United States, and such other studies as may be prescribed by rule or regulation of the state board of education. All teachers shall stress the importance of the cultiviation of manners, the fundamental principles of honesty, honor, industry and economy, the minimum requisites for good health including the beneficial effect of physical exercise, and the worth of kindness to all living creatures.

28A.03.300     Purpose in screening for learning and language disabilities

The legislature recognizes as its initial duty in carrying out its responsibility to see to the education of the children of this state the importance of screening children within the schools to determine if there be any of such children with learning/language disabilities. It is the intent and purpose of RCW 28A.03.320 to identify the number of children with recognizable learning/language disabilities, the type thereof, and to determine educational methods appropriate thereto (Added by Laws 1st Ex Sess 1975, Chapter 78, Section 1, effective May 26, 1975.)

28A.03.310    Program duties prescribed in screening

The superintendent of public instruction shall, by rule or regulation in accordance with chapter 34.04 RCW, adopt a program under which all public schools within the state carrying out an elementary school program shall implement an appropriate screening device designed to identify children with learning/language disabilities to be administered to first grade students prior to their entrance into the second grade. After approval by the superintendent, or his designee, of any such appropriate screening device offered by a particular school, such screening shall be administered not later than January 1, 1976.

29A.03.360    Achievement level surveys: scope, purpose, procedure

(1) It shall be the intent and purpose of this section to direct the office of superintendent of public instruction to conduct standardized reading, mathematics, and language arts achievement level surveys of approximately two thousand students distributed throughout the state in each of the grade levels of this section. The survey testing shall be based on a statistical random sample of students from these grade levels sufficient to generalize about all of the students at each of the selected grade levels from the state's school districts. The purpose of these surveys is to allow the public and the legislature to evaluate how Washington students in these grades compare to students in the same grades tested in other comparable national achievement surveys. The office of superintendent of public instruction shall coordinate such tests and provide such information as obtained therefrom to the legislature no less often than once every four years.

(2) The superintendent of public instruction shall prepare a report to the legislature on the achievement level surveys conducted in the 1975-77 biennium and for each of the subsequent testing cycles as designated by the superintendent of public instruction's office. Such report shall include a comparison of the achievement levels attained by Washington students to the levels attained by students outside of the state, with special emphasis placed on the basic skills of reading, mathematics, and language arts. Such report shall also focus on appropriate input variables and comparisons of variables reported by other states' testing programs.

(3) Results of the first survey test shall be made available to the school districts and the legislature no later than June 30, 1977.

(4) In addition to the survey testing for grades eight and eleven as set forth in this section, every school district is encouraged to test pupils in grade two by an assessment device designed or selected by the local school districts. This test shall be used to help teachers in

identifying those pupils in need of assistance in the skills of reading, writing, mathematics, and language arts. The test results are not to be compiled by the superintendent of public instruction, but are only to be used by the local school district.

(5) The superintendent of public instruction shall prepare, with the assistance of local school districts, and conduct a standardized achievement test to be given annually to all pupils in grade four. The test shall assess students' skill in reading, mathematics, and language arts and shall focus upon appropriate input variables. Results of such tests shall be compiled by the superintendent of public instruction, who shall make those results available annually to the legislature, to all local school districts and subsequently to parents of those children tested. The results shall allow parents to ascertain the achievement levels and input variables of their children as compared with the other students within the district, the state and, if applicable, the nation (Added by Laws 2nd Ex Sess 1975-76, Chapter 98, Section 1, effective July 1, 1976.)

## WEST VIRGINIA

No code provision found.

## WISCONSIN

118:01     Public instruction

(1) Fundamental course: Reading, writing, spelling, English grammar and composition, geography, arithmetic, elements of agriculture and conservation of natural resources, history and civil government of the United States and of Wisconsin, citizenship and such other subjects as the school board determines shall be taught in every elementary school. All instruction shall be in the English language, except that the school board may cause any foreign language to be taught to such pupils as desire it.

## WISCONSIN

199.22     Curriculum requirements (refers to Milwaukee schools)

(1) Elementary schools: Courses in reading, writing, spelling, English, grammar and composition, geography, arithmetic, elements of

agriculture and . . . conservation of natural resources, history and civil government of the United States and of Wisconsin, physical education, sanitation, physiology and hygiene, the effects of controlled substances under Chapter 161 and alcohol upon the human system, symptoms of disease, proper care of the body and such other subjects as the board determines shall be included in the course of study in elementary schools in order to obtain the objectives identified by the board under Section 119.16(1). If his parent files with the teacher written objection thereto, no pupil is required to take instruction in physiology and hygiene, in the effects of controlled substances and alcohol and in symptoms of disease.

(2) High schools: Courses in arithmetic, sciences, business and commerce, civics, English, languages, history, mathematics, physical training and such other subjects as the board determines shall be taught in the high schools in order to obtain the objectives identified by the board under Section 119:16(1).

# WYOMING

No code provisions found.